DON'T BLAME IT ON RIO

DON'T BLAME IT ON RIO

*The Real Deal
Behind Why
Men Go to Brazil
for Sex*

By Jewel Woods

and Karen Hunter

GRAND CENTRAL
PUBLISHING

NEW YORK   BOSTON

The names and other identifying characteristics of the people who shared their stories with the author have been changed.

Grand Central Publishing
Hachette Book Group USA
237 Park Avenue
New York, NY 10017

Visit our Web site at www.HachetteBookGroupUSA.com.

Printed in the United States of America

First Edition: April 2008
10 9 8 7 6 5 4 3 2 1

Grand Central Publishing is a division of Hachette Book Group USA, Inc. The Grand Central Publishing name and logo is a trademark of Hachette Book Group USA, Inc.

Library of Congress Cataloging-in-Publication Data

Woods, Jewel.
    Don't blame it on Rio: the real deal behind why men go to Brazil for sex / Jewel Woods and Karen Hunter. —1st ed.
        p. cm.
    ISBN-13: 978-0-446-17806-8
    ISBN-10: 0-446-17806-3
    1. Sex tourism—Brazil. 2. Adultery—United States. I. Hunter, Karen. II. Title.
    HQ173.W66 2008
    306.74'20981—dc22
                                                                        2007041319

Book design by Charles Sutherland

To professional black men who struggle to find meaning in their lives, and to professional black women who continue to love them despite the pain and heartache it causes.

Also to the next generation of boys who will hopefully grow into adult men that our ancestors dreamed about and that black women need and deserve.

Finally, this book is dedicated to Thelma Smith, the woman I thank God for every day and whom I miss so much.

Acknowledgments

I want to thank the men who agreed to tell their stories. Without your candor, I would not have had the opportunity to explore men's lives the way I have sought to in this book. Although I am certain you will not agree with *all* of my findings, I hope what I shared reflects what was spoken and unspoken in the numerous conversations over the years.

I want to thank New Voices for granting me a fellowship that allowed me to do this work. It is because of that support that I now look forward to building a multi-cultural, multi-issue men's organization that truly influences the lives of men and boys everywhere.

To the men in Michigan and Ohio, whom I have had the pleasure of working with and for over the years, thank you. Special thanks to Rafael, Brett, Dominick, Lincoln, Carlton, Vince, Steve, and David.

I also want to thank the extraordinary mentors I have acquired over the years, like Dr. Rich Tolman, Dr. Celia Williamson, Dr. Vincent Diaz, Dr. A.G. Miller, Dr. Rubin Patterson, Diane, Linda, Moe, and Peggy.

Thanks to my homies: Dave, Vince, Leslie. Special thanks to Dr. Larry Clark, who has been there supporting me since the beginning. This book is intellectually indebted to six writers, whose projects have deeply shaped my thinking: Jamaica Kincaid, Orlando Patterson, Barbara Ehrenreich, Philippe Bourgois, Patillo McCoy, and Clyde Franklin II.

Special thanks to Dr. Thaddeus Blanchette, a brilliant anthropologist and activist working in Rio, who has influenced my thinking about the issues of men and sex tourism. Thanks also to the activists and intellectuals who work in the domestic and sexual violence movement. These are awesome men and women who do inspiring work every day.

To the writer who has been instrumental in this project, Lady K. (Karen Hunter). Some may never know about your passion and your commitment to black people, but I do. Thanks for everything!

To my editor, Karen Thomas, and the entire Grand Central Publishing/Hachette team, thank you for believing in this project and giving your all to make it successful. And to Ian Kleinert, my agent, thank you, too, for getting the vision and making it happen.

Thanks and love to my immediate family: my mother, Cassandra; my sister, Tanisha; and my nephews, Jason and Javon.

Finally to the three individuals who give my life meaning, structure, dignity, and grace: my wife, Abena; my daughter, Akua; and my son, Azikiwe. I hope that I give as much as I receive.

Contents

DON'T BLAME IT ON RIO

Preface

Are Black Women Necessary?

If professional black women gave black men what we really needed and wanted, there would be no need for us to go over (to Brazil or anyplace else).

There are plenty of black women here who are single. But being single and being professional just ain't enough. Most professional black men feel that they can spend their own money. What I'm looking for from a woman is something totally different.

Some women call us chauvinistic or old school, or something like that. You hear (women) talking all the time about what's happening out here. They say that men can't be trusted, men cheat, they're no good. They look outward; they never look within themselves to see what they are doing. They never ask what they need to change.

It doesn't take much for a decent professional man to get married. Any professional black man can get married. I can find a wife. But is it that I want? And the thing that I noticed about myself, in taking these pilgrimages to Brazil and the Dominican Republic, is that I've lost patience with a lot of black women in America. I'm serious, man. Sometimes I go out with women and they are totally into me and then they start doing things that just kind of annoy me that probably would not have annoyed before because my objective was so clear to make this into something. I don't have that level of patience now; I now want to be served. I want to be treated the way I need to be treated—mentally, physically, sexually.

I would like to have a significant relationship (with a sister in America). But if I have to compromise, I'm just not willing to do it. I can't. Not when I can just export me one from Brazil who will take care of me if I bring her here!

—Isaac, 41, attorney, Philadelphia

Black women were once at the center of black men's lives, as wives, mothers, lovers, and partners. As late as the 1960s, more than 60 percent of black adults were married. However, in this generation, black women have become somewhat of a nuisance, a burden, and perhaps even a pariah in black men's lives. In contrast to the times when it was illegal in some places for black men even to look at white women—a time when there was a commitment to the black family, and black men really didn't have many choices—today, black men like Isaac have choices, and they are taking full advantage of them.

By most accounts, Isaac is a "good man." He is highly educated and gainfully employed. He is a "good catch." He is part of that "talented 13 percent" of black males with a college degree. But what he is expressing, while disturbing, is something many black men are feeling today. He doesn't want to be bothered. Isaac doesn't want to have to work to have a relationship. And he feels that being in a relationship with a black woman in America is a lot of work. It's a sentiment shared by Jermain, an educator in Memphis, Tennessee:

> *Black women are more demanding. And demanding in a way—not an awful way—that I can't fulfill. I feel I would need two of me to make any black woman happy. I've got to give her* all *my time,* all *my attention. But what about me? I need the head cheerleader to build me up when I'm having a bad day. (The black woman) seems to always need us to be there for her.*
>
> *I'm only one man. And I'm a man. (And I do believe that men and women are different.) I'm not naturally a sharer. I have a very happy life. I have good friends; I have a job I enjoy. When I come home, I rest and relax, eat dinner, watch a little TV, maybe go out. So when she comes home and is like, "I've had the worst day ever, blahblahblahblah . . . ," sometimes I don't want to hear that. But you've got to support them all the time. I have bad days, too, and I don't feel like she has to listen to me talk about it all the time. I just find black women demanding to a point where—excuse me, sorry—that it's difficult to deal with them on a twenty-four-hour, seven-day basis.*

We could choose to view Isaac's and Jermain's opinions as isolated, but the statistics would be hard to ignore. In 1960 62 percent of black males were married; in 2000 it was only 43 percent—a trend, it could be argued, that is due to the decline in jobs among black men. However, the fact is that marriage rates also declined for black males with jobs during this period. And more important, affluent black males are no more likely to be married than poor black men.

The result for African-American women is a precipitous increase in the percentage of those who have never married from around 36 percent to 62 percent between 1950 and 2000. The picture becomes even bleaker if you focus on black women and consider that at the very time that the marriage rates have declined, the 1990s witnessed an unprecedented number of interracial marriages among blacks. According to the most recent reports, the 1990s saw a decrease in interracial marriage rates among most racial and ethnic groups. The one exception? African-Americans. Specifically, there was a decline in intermarriage rates among Hispanics, Asian, and Native Americans with whites. In contrast, black men largely drove the increase in interracial marriages with whites. Black men married to white women outnumber black women married to white men almost three to one (14 percent versus 5 percent, respectively).

The trends further demonstrate that black men of every socioeconomic category increased their rate of interracial marriages, with some of the largest increases among black men with less than a high school education. So the problem is not just that there aren't enough good black men around to commit and to marry black women, but rather that the "good" black men are choosing *not* to get married or to remarry.

Isaac was very clear on the idea that he could marry a professional black woman if he wanted to. But what he was "looking for was something totally different."

The other problem is that when black men do choose to marry, a disproportionate number of them choose *not* to marry black women. Some will suggest that despite the increase in African-Americans involved in interracial marriages, the number still constitutes a small minority of marriages and does not explain what is happening in relationships between black men and women. In 1980 only 120,000 black males were married to white women. By 2000 that number had more than doubled. In isolation, these trends of decreased marriage rates, increased interracial rates, and increased never-married rates don't explain what is happening between black men and black women. However, they do highlight the paradox of why so many black men travel overseas to find a woman when there are so many seemingly eligible, beautiful black women right in their own backyard. Here is what Thomas, a consultant in Fort Lauderdale, Florida, said:

> *I'm in my fifties now; the first time I went to Rio, I was in my thirties. And what essentially drove me to Rio was being sick and tired of not only being placed in a box by our own women and the media . . . but, essentially just the feeling or the need to search for what I thought, in my mind, was what I was supposed to receive as a successful black man moving forward in the way of relationship with a woman.*

For the first time ever, large and growing numbers of black men have the option to ask what they perceive to be a legitimate question: Are black women necessary? This is a question that has become even more remarkable given the economic class of black men who have an unprecedented amount of exposure and access to black women and other women. These black men are financially stable, and they have the financial resources and disposable income that allow them to explore new social and sexual frontiers filled with exotic and erotic women. But one need not be rich to participate in this new reality. As Thomas noted, "You could be making thirty-five thousand and go over there and have plenty of money. That's why you see a lot of the fifty-year-olds that retire getting their pension of two to three thousand a month just going ahead and moving to Brazil."

Clearly, one of the most powerful and enduring dynamics about Brazilian women in the minds of black men is that they offer the best of both black women and white women. Brazilian and other so-called Third World women possess the physical bodies and sexuality of black women—and, according to men, even more—while at the same time they have the attitudes, femininity, and worldviews of white women. One person referred to Brazilian women as the "kryptonite" to black women.

In the famous words of a Brazilian scholar, they are "neither black nor white." And because they are neither black nor white, they provide the ultimate contrast to the idea of what black women are not. This is different from the fantasies black men used to have about white women. Years ago Frantz Fanon could write, "When my restless hands caress those white breasts, they grasp White Civilization and dignity and make them mine," or Eldridge Cleaver could reportedly rape light-skinned black women as a form of practice on his way up to white women. These fantasies were mainly about power and what was historically denied to black men.

The relationships that black men have with Brazilian and other Third World women is about: (1) *Recognition*, where black men see in themselves something that they think has been lost in black women. What Brazilian women in particular, and other so-called Third World women in general, offer is an idea of what has been lost in the past and what could be in the future. (2) *Reverence*, where men of a certain class can gain access to a way of life that they think they deserve because of their status. The result is a dynamic that allows for a wide spectrum of black men, from conservatives to leftist progressives, all the way to the Afrocentrics, to find what they think they are missing in black women. Here is how another successful black professional man described the attraction of Brazilian women:

> *When you compare black American women to Brazilian women, even though she is not at your level, you don't feel like she is below your level. You feel like she is more of a support system than [competition]. That's the distinction. You don't want to be in a race with somebody; you don't want to feel as though they are a hindrance. You want to feel like, "Wow, this person really supports me."*
>
> *Making the bed, taking care of the kids, keeping food on the table, taking care of me in the bed. What else do I need? I find that guys want it all. We really do want it all. If we can get a women that is career oriented, yet she does the things we expect a woman to do—maintain the household, etc.—that*

would be a grand package. But let's be honest. If we had the choice between a Stepford wife and someone who is constantly challenging us, a Stepford wife would more than likely win. Imagine having the looks and she is a bit of servant, too. I think that is the appeal of Brazil. You are getting them both!

As an African-American male who has dedicated his life to safety and security within the African-American community, it is important that I share what I have learned from men over the past several years.

This book is not only going to deal with the question "Are black women necessary?" It will also take a look at the broader question of why black men are looking for something they think is outside black women and whether professional black men really do want subordinate women or "Stepford wives." It is an opportunity to examine what black people must do to repair the damage that has taken more than three hundred years of slavery—which was the first rip at the black family—all the way through Jim Crow and beyond, to arrive at this somber place.

The reality is that African-American men didn't just wake up one day and decide that black women, once the center of their identities as husbands, fathers of their children, lovers, and partners, are now exchangeable. They also didn't just pick up and travel thousands of miles to Brazil, the Dominican Republic, Panama, the Philippines, and a host of other places "just to pay for sex."

The good news is that from this discussion and examination, black men and women can come to some solutions and perhaps some hope that there can be a future for black men and black women. Out of this discussion, perhaps women can gain some valuable insights into the minds and actions of black men, and perhaps black men can look in the mirror and see how hurtful they often are and change their behaviors. Maybe this can help black men change their perspectives and change the way their actions and attitudes are tearing down the black woman and thus the entire black family.

Like the man who pronounced boldly, "I have never had one black woman treat me as well as the worst woman in Brazil." This is a statement that both women and men must process and grow from.

This is a unique opportunity for the men in the black community to talk about the root causes, because it's not the black woman. It's a chance to talk about oppression as well as the privileges many have. No other class of men is doing what these men now have an opportunity to do. For so long, African-American men have been the anti-example—the example of what *not* to be. This is a historic opportunity for black men to show not only America but also people of color around the world that they are not just the typical "ugly American." In fact, these men can do what America in general seems unable to do: save the black family!

In 2005 *New York Times* columnist Maureen Dowd wrote a book titled *Are Men Necessary?* It was an exploration into sexual politics from a white female perspective. Dowd argued that what men really want are subordinate women.

In this book we answer her questions and raise more. I attempt to give the real reason why men are making trips overseas for women—women they claim they can't find at home. At a minimum, black men make trips overseas for physical reasons that include sex. However, many have experienced a level of physical and sexual intimacy, a sort of sexual healing, that they see as lacking in many of their current relationships with black women. They also make these trips for cultural reasons. They describe a deep embrace and recognition of a people, a time, and a land that they do not get here in the United States and do not see in black women. Most important, these men increasingly travel overseas because of a profound sense of identity that they find and create on these trips. So what they ultimately end up paying for is access to an elite male experience, and intercourse with a set of beliefs and ideas about black manhood that they think are denied them in America. The problem is that during these journeys, sometimes consciously but also unconsciously, black men are led further away from black women—not just physically but also emotionally, psychologically, and spiritually.

In an attempt to understand and sometimes justify their actions, these men also begin to develop some sophisticated, demeaning, and denigrating ideas about black women in the process. The result: many African-American men do not see black women in the roles that they did during the times when a commitment to the black family was less a matter of choice. In the end, their conclusion is that black women are no longer necessary.

I will show them why they are wrong!

Introduction

Biggest Secret in Black America: The Lowdown on the _Other_ Down Low

There's this comedian and he was on Howard Stern. And he was talking about how he went to Brazil to get women. He was talking about how much easier it was for him to just go down there and meet women and not have to worry about all of the stuff he has to deal with here.

Then I was talking to one of my friends and he's in a fraternity. And we're just talking about things and he was saying he wanted to go to Brazil—he and some of his fraternity brothers. And I just thought that was really weird because [I started to] think, "What is up with Brazil?"

—Sharon, 37, African-American, office manager

Brazil. Rio. Tall and tan and young and lovely. Her name was Lola; she was a showgirl . . . They've been singing about her, writing about her, fantasizing about the Brazilian woman for decades. In the black community, though, she is the biggest, worst-kept secret. Black men, particularly middle-class, successful black men, know someone who has gone to Brazil, desire to go, or have been there themselves.

Traveling to Brazil for sex and sanctuary is so prevalent that it has become an inside joke. It was a secret only to black women. And it was a secret to some poor black men because they couldn't afford to make the trip. But it was a secret being lived out in plain view. I have to admit, if not for my research and work with black men as a social worker who has counseled hundreds of men, I might have been left out of the secret, too. I knew about the intrigue surrounding trips to Brazil, but I didn't know how prevalent it really was until I was standing in line at a local Detroit pizza shop. I was about to order pizza, and I struck up a conversation with the manager, who was behind the counter. He was an average-looking guy, dressed in a long-sleeved white shirt and dark slacks. There was nothing remarkable about his appearance. He was either in his late twenties or early thirties, and he had a small diamond ring on his pinkie finger. The shop was relatively empty. There was staff, but they were far enough away from earshot not to be able to overhear anything we said. There was no one behind me in line, either, so I figured, what the hell. I asked him the same question that I had been asking other black men for months.

"Hey, brother," I said. "My name is Jewel Woods, and I work in a program for black men, and we're talking with brothers who have traveled overseas, particularly to Brazil. Do you know anyone who has been to Brazil?"

His answer sadly confirmed what I suspected and feared, and what I was desperately trying to understand.

Not only did he know someone who had gone to Brazil, but he also had a friend who had married a woman from Brazil. He had also heard all the stories of black men going to Brazil to, in his words, "Go buck wild!"

Certainly, it could be the case that I just happened to be in the one pizza parlor where the one black, male manager not only just happened to have heard of black men going to Brazil, but also knew of someone who had married a Brazilian woman. Or it could be that this phenomenon of black men (and others) going overseas to live the lifestyle of kings was as widespread as I had come to believe it was, but that nobody was talking about it publicly.

I remember that feeling I had when that manager revealed that he knew about Brazil, because it was the third time I had that feeling. I was not just surprised; I was also a little disgusted. I know the statistics of the numbers of black women who are dealing with the prospect of living their lives out alone or, worse, dealing with a cheating or abusive man for lack of options. I know how hard sisters work to take care of the household and the kids and keep the family together. That men, black men, are so carefree, so willing just to go overseas and have sex—often very risky sex—and not even consider what it might be doing to their wives, girlfriends, or community was heartbreaking. And added to that was the notion that black men were taking advantage of women of color in another country who had limited options and were prostituting themselves not because they wanted to but for survival.

The first time I experienced this was when an academic colleague of mine had come over to visit for the holidays, and in our "catching up" and sharing, he started to talk about the recent trip he had made to Brazil. The moment he started to disclose all the things he did, my immediate reaction was to challenge him on his behavior.

My reaction made him clam up. He was reluctant to continue the conversation. But what it started for me was a process of questioning. How was it possible that this brilliant, politically informed brother could be participating in what I thought was such obviously destructive and exploitative behavior toward other people of color?

But I had to back up and think. I had to process what was really happening here. There was a larger question. Why did he and other professional black men—supposedly the most coveted men in the community—have to go all the way to Brazil to find women who satisfied them? In many ways, it was that situation and those questions that compelled me to want to learn more about this.

The second time I had that feeling was September 17, 2004. I remember the date because I immediately e-mailed myself. At that moment, I was in the bathroom with my two-year-old waiting for her to "finish her business," when I heard a famous comedian go into his routine on the *Tom Joyner Morning Show*. It was a routine I had heard him give before about how being with one person in a relationship was something like having only selected channels when cable was available; only this time he included in his bit something along the lines of "I went to Brazil and had, like, fifteen J-Lo's for an apple and some M and Ms."

I remember being thunderstruck because I had just started talking seriously with other professional black men who had gone to Brazil, and here it was being announced publicly. It was shortly thereafter that I began to understand that it was a classic insider's joke. But how big an "inside joke" was it? How many professional black men were actually participating in this phenomenon? I set out on a quest to find the answers. I began talking with black men from various backgrounds and from various regions of America. Most of these men were middle class to wealthy. But they all had a similar experience in their dealings in Brazil.

What I came away with was that Brazil was becoming more and more popular and that there were many more men traveling there than I ever imagined. According to Mediamark Research, which collects travel data, over the last three years approximately 1.6 million African-American men have traveled to a foreign country. There is an estimated 98,000 traveling to Central and South America each year. Those with college degrees were two times more likely to travel overseas compared with those that only graduated from high school, and those with postgraduate degrees were four times more likely to travel overseas than those with high school degrees. In addition, African-American men who were married were more likely to have traveled overseas than either African-American men who were never married or African-American men who were legally separated/widowed/or divorced.

There are so many black men who travel to Brazil that they have clubs and online chat rooms devoted to the experience. There have even been quite a few well-publicized scandals. In one incident, a group of twenty-nine men, along with forty prostitutes, were arrested on a boat in Rio. Here is how the news was sent out over one of the popular message boards and lit up the forums:

Dear xxx & xxx members, this message is to inform you of some recent developments in Rio de Janeiro that may affect your travel plans. Last night June 11, 2005–29 Americans were arrested and are being deported for suspected "Sexual Tourism" and drugs, and also without having identification on them. This is a front-page story in Brazil's largest newspaper O'Globo and on the News. The group of 29 Americans were on a boat called the Shangrila along with 40 prostitutes. Brazilian Federal Police who have been investigating operators of sexual tourism intercepted the boat in the Marina da Gloria. The organizer of the event, an American, xxx & xxx who has had problems in the past with this kind of "boat ride," has been arrested and is being held on accusations of running a sexual tourism agency. His photo has appeared in Brazilian newspapers and TV news. The other Americans are being deported within 3 days and will have their visas revoked and not be able to return to Brazil. All the women involved are regulars of the Help/Mia Pataca scene. They were released with incident. [e-mail sent to me, edited]

By most accounts, the majority of the men on the boat were African-American. In another incident, allegedly forty men, all African-American, were arrested and then deported:

Last week, police raided Termas Rio Antigo in the Lapa district. Approximately 40 were arrested, including the girls working at the Termas. They were shown on the Brazilian TV station, Rede Record, being led out in handcuffs. [e-mail sent to me, edited]

The peculiar thing, according to this report, is that while the Brazilian women were handcuffed with their hands in front so they could cover their faces while the TV cameras rolled, black Americans were handcuffed with their hands behind their backs so that their faces could be seen. The newscaster commented that all the men were African-Americans and that they were the number one sexual tourist group coming to Brazil.

The girls were held at the police station until their parents picked them up. One of the girls was the daughter of a federal deputy. The men were all deported back to the United States, according to the report.

The reason Termas was raided, according to the report, was because of prostitution and sexual tourism. But the real reason that this raid happened is because Termas's owners didn't pay off the police in order to stay open, the report added.

The idea that African-American men are the number one sex tourists is false and the product of both "prejudice and ignorance," according to Thaddeus Blanchette, Ph.D., an expert who studies sex tourism in Rio. However, he says that the raids do illustrate how the authorities are targeting African-American men to cut down on sexual tourism.

Now, where else in the world can you find a group of more than twenty professional black men on a boat with prostitutes unless the men are on a professional sports team? And how in the world can all this be going on and no one be aware of it? Was it simply an inside joke, or did the lack of conversation about these issues say more about how good these men are at keeping this information hidden from each other—or how good a community is at keeping information hidden from itself?

The African-American community has a strong history of protecting itself and providing shelter and sanctuary for its members. It also has a history of protecting itself from harm from the outside society by being very selective with how it chooses to deal with certain issues. Because of the pain, embarrassment, and trauma of how information has been historically used against blacks, they have been especially wary of talking about things in public. Thus, the idea of "not airing dirty laundry" or speaking "within the veil," for fear of how it will be used against blacks by the wider society, is well known. The result is often that blacks don't discuss things, because we are painfully aware of the costs of airing dirty laundry. The problem is that by not having certain conversations, we are potentially not doing the work of attending to certain wounds that need to be aired in order to heal. Discussing things is the first step toward solutions.

There are some obvious reasons, however, why this whole notion of black men traveling overseas for sex has flown under the radar. The most obvious reason is because it happens so far away. It's sort of like "What happens in Vegas stays in Vegas"— what goes on in Brazil and the Dominican Republic and Thailand stays there. These men are very selective about how they choose to share the actual details of their experiences.

So men lie. They lie to the ladies in their lives, or they take the "don't ask, don't tell approach." At the group level, black men tell well-coordinated lies to accommodate the planning and the covering up of their trips upon their return home. When the truth does come out and a wife or significant other does discover what's really going on, it often ends in tragedy. One wife who found out about her husband traveling abroad posed online in one of the chat rooms and "outed" her husband and his friends.

But they never tell. They never betray the fraternity of men who travel overseas for sex and sanctuary. Because once the cat is out of the bag, they will have some serious explaining to do.

Well, we are officially letting the cat out of the bag! In this book we will unveil some of the secrets that men have been keeping to themselves for years about their experiences overseas. But it's not to out them. My goal is to heal the black community. And if we can't talk about it, we can't fix it. And if men still don't want to answer to some of the behaviors that I will be showing in this book, at least black women will be armed. Because knowledge is power. And what you don't know can hurt you.

Black people are always struggling to get to the root of our issues. We will talk and argue, but sometimes we don't get at the heart of the matter. The black community chooses to deal with sex and sexuality according to class. This is not a class issue. This is a sexuality issue. And on a deeper level, it's an abuse issue. The middle- and upper-class blacks feel that the ills that plague our community only plague the lower class. They believe that the problems start and stem there, that "those" people are making it hard for the rest of us by projecting these negative images.

So when we talk about AIDS and HIV, it becomes "their problem." It's a drug addict issue or a gay issue, so it's not my issue, they think. The conversations surrounding men being on the "down low," which sparked heated debate and conversation within the black community, was a perfect example of this. At its core were elements that are always fascinating: sex, deceit, black men, and death. Eventually, that conversation led to the publication of numerous articles and several books. JL King's *On the Down Low: Journey into the Lives of "Straight" Black Men Who Sleep with Men* and Keith Boykin's *Beyond the Down Low* were perhaps the two most important.

The discourse surrounding the "down low" accomplished a number of things, but perhaps the two most important were (1) it raised the level of awareness of HIV and AIDS in the black community to a certain degree; and (2) it offered a complex and sensitive portrait of the issues that gay and bisexual black men face, in ways that were never discussed before.

However, a number of problems came as a result of that conversation.

Most important, the discourse surrounding the "down low" excluded the vast majority of black men in the community. The majority of that conversation involved only gay and/or bisexual men, many of whom often had to defend themselves against angry and frightened black women. As a result, the majority of black men in the community—those who were heterosexual (simply defined as not having sex with other men)—did not participate in that conversation at all. In fact, not only did the vast majority of black men not participate, it effectively gave the majority of black men a "free pass" because it confirmed in their minds, just as in most people's minds, that abhorrent or deviant sexual practices were specific to gay and bisexual men.

So "straight" black men got let off the hook. By having all the focus put on the sexual practices of gay and bisexual black men, heterosexual black men were able to point the finger and say in a nonreflective way, "Ah ha! See, it is the sexual behaviors of those gay and bisexual men that are putting the black community at risk—not *my* behavior."

But let this be the first place it's said: heterosexual men are just as responsible, if not more responsible, for putting the black community at risk!

Yes, despite that "down low" behavior at its core is risky and hidden, what straight men are up to is far more dangerous, because they are never suspected.

Even when there was an attempt to presumably broaden the conversation and have open and honest "down low" dialogue about how it was affecting the black community—and particularly black women—the focus effectively exempted heterosexual black men. Boykin, who offered the most complex reading of the issues on that point, was unintentionally guilty of this. Early in his book he offered seven different profiles of people who were involved in complex social and sexual situations, and then asked the question, "Which of the people mentioned above are on the down low?"

His point was to show how hard it was to specifically define what "down low" was. The problem was that none of the seven examples or profiles was of men we would normally define as "straight" or heterosexual. So by default, this type of framing or conceptualizing of "down low" excluded the majority of men from any of the nuanced conversation about sex, sexuality, and disclosure that he was aiming for.

Again, I don't think this was intentional, but it is interesting and alarming to think that we can have honest and open conversations about sex and sexuality when less than half the community is ever involved. Consequently, the images of sexually abhorrent or deviant behavior to emerge were consistent with the images of pedophiles or the gay and bisexual black male booty snatchers.

How can we talk about these issues when we don't even think about sex and sexuality the same way? Where do we start? Sociologist Orlando Patterson was one of the first to highlight some of the "significant" differences between black men and women around issues of sex and sexuality. Using data from the National Health and Social Life Survey (NHSLS), which at the time was the most authoritative data on such issues, Patterson pointed out that 30 percent of all black men condoned sex with a complete stranger, while only around 8 percent of black women thought it was okay. There was a sixteen-point gap between middle-class black men and women on the issue of teenage sex and a twenty-point gap in beliefs about premarital sex. In the area of extramarital affairs, 92 percent of black women said that extramarital sex is wrong, compared to only 72 percent of black men. In addition, Patterson showed that black men and women differ in attitudes and beliefs about such sexual practices as cunnilingus and fellatio.

He found so many differences that he pondered, "Considering the marked differences in sexual values between African-American men and women, one is led to wonder what goes on between them when they actually get together."

The cumulative result of that "down low" conversation was the perpetuation of a narrow and parochial way of defining risky sexual behavior, which obscured other significant trends and issues within the black community, such as divorce, separation, and never-married rates, that are indicative of profound social, economic, and political differences between black men and women.

So while we are redefining this "down low" discussion as not merely a gay problem, here's the newsflash: HIV/AIDS is now the leading cause of death among blacks between the ages of twenty-five and forty-four. All blacks! Straight blacks. Black women. It's not drugs, homicide, or heart disease. It's HIV and AIDS!

We don't talk about the recent studies of thirty-two states

between 2000 and 2003 showing that only half of gay black men with HIV are infected through homosexual sex (compared to 72 percent of white men). But 80 percent of black women affected with HIV contracted it through heterosexual sex. Does this suggest that HIV in the black community is mainly a heterosexual disease? In other words, has the most intimate act between heterosexual black men and women become potentially the most lethal?

It should come as no surprise that we rarely discuss the black middle class in this country, period—let alone its risky sexual behavior. It is even rarer, that we discuss middle-class and professional black men. According to the Bureau of Labor Statistics, in 2005 there were approximately 23,000 black male physicians, 26,000 black male lawyers, more than 40,000 black male engineers, and several more thousands of black male dentists, certified public accountants, and other professionals. In 2005 there were 1,502,000 black men listed in management, professional, and related occupations. Yet we know virtually nothing about professional black male lives aside from athletes and entertainers.

Middle-class and professional black men are, in effect, "the invisible men" in the community. In contrast, almost all the popular images of black male identity and masculinity are of urban, street, and underclass black man. However, black professional masculine identity is not expressed by the likes of Lil' Wayne, Lil' Scrappy, Dem Franchise Boys, Mike Jones, Nelly, 50 Cent, or the Snoop Dogg types. In fact, most public expressions of professional black masculinity are in stark contrast to urban street masculinity. Aside from athletes and entertainers, black professionals can ill afford to wear grilles, cornrows, or tattoos.

The same type of erasure of black professional masculinity that occurs in popular society also occurs in academic research. There is virtually no academic research on professional black men. Similar to what has happened in popular culture, almost all the academic research on black men is of poor and working poor black men. One consequence of this absence and invisibility is that any discussion of "negative" behaviors of black men in the community is almost always aimed at the poor. Whether as victims of racism or as resilient agents in their own lives, the poor and working poor receive the majority of attention in the black community. The result is that the ideas, beliefs, and behaviors of the middle and professional class, particularly of black men, is rarely discussed or scrutinized.

The debate surrounding the *New York Times* article titled, "Plight Deepens for Black Men, Studies Warn" was another good illustration of this. The article pointed to a litany of studies by experts at Columbia, Harvard, Princeton, Georgetown, and institutions such as the Urban Institute—all pointing to a "dire situation" for poor young black men, the majority of whom, according to the article, "are becoming ever more disconnected from the mainstream of society."

I remember the op-ed pieces, the national conference at the University of Pennsylvania called "Poor, Young, Black And Male: A Case for National Action," and the *Washington Post* starting a year-long series titled "On Being a Black Man" shortly thereafter.

What I recall the most, however, was an op-ed by the brilliant activist Kevin Powell in the *New York Post*, emphasizing the responsibility of professional black men to be mentors and guides to other black men:

> *I issue a challenge to professional, successful Black males like myself: Become a breathing, living example for these poor Black boys and men. Share life lessons with them, mentor them, please, and do not be afraid of them, ever. And have the courage, the vision . . .*

The thought that kept running through my mind as I was reading this was, "If professional black men are going to save poor and working poor black men, who is going to save professional black men?"

There was no sense surrounding that discussion—or any that followed—that professional black men could actually be part of the problem. There was no acknowledgment that perhaps the reason why it might be so dark in the lives of poor and working poor black men is because no light has been shed on the lives of middle-class and professional black men.

There was no acknowledgment that for some black men, those who have been able to find themselves in a veritable sea of opportunity when it comes to women, life is very good.

Another example of a refusal to see just how class differences work among black men was the recent finding by the Kaiser Foundation and the *Washington Post* that eight out of ten black men said they were satisfied with their lives, while six out of ten said that it was a good time to be a black man in the United States.

Reportedly, Bill Cosby had so many problems with this finding that he referred to the editors of the *Washington Post* series as "Judases."

Even when reality is staring us in the face about the complexities and contradictions of class in the black community, we choose not to see it. The fact is that certain questions are not asked of black middle-class men so they are also largely hidden. If you were to take that same group of middle-class and professional black men who go to conferences ostensibly to solve the problems of poor and working poor black men off to the side and make them talk about their infidelity issues, their divorce issues, their black-women issues, their white-people-at-the-job issues, they'd probably pass out.

The real "down low" in black America today has to do not just with what black men are doing sexually behind closed doors and overseas. It has to do with what largely remains hidden in the hearts and minds of "good black men" in the community, who increasingly see black women and America as places where they can't get what they need.

The real down low has to do with the profound significance and meaning attached to these experiences in the minds and memories of black men. For professional black men, Brazil raises the question of morality, masculinity, and male privilege in ways that have never been raised before.

The conversations of black men in this book demonstrate more than anything that professional black men, "men of means," take advantage of their class status to live the lifestyles that they feel are denied to them in America by whites and by black women. And for black women, it is this real down low behavior that they aren't even checking for. But this is the down low behavior that could be killing them.

Given what I have chosen to do with my life, which is to focus on the lives of men, I have the unique opportunity to examine, explore, and, yes, expose aspects of black male life that put men at risk of both "victimizing" and "victimization." Chances are, I will be accused of selling brothers out, exposing the one spot on the planet where brothers can go and exhale—even though it's clear that brothers are doing way more than just exhaling. I might even be accused of being jealous because I can't go, or of being guilty of "pathologizing" black men and making them look different from other men.

As for selling out, we men have got to start telling on each other and ourselves. The connection between masculinity, morality, and male privilege has never been more important. And someone has got to talk about it. In terms of exposing the one place on earth where, seemingly, brothers can exhale and be treated like men, isn't it a fundamental contradiction that joy and happiness can be built on so much poverty and misery? I mean, look at where they are going for this so-called pleasure. And look at who is really being exploited.

In terms of pathologizing black men, just the opposite is true. All you have to do is look at the HBO series *Rome* and the movie *300* to know that black people, and black men specifically, don't have the monopoly on immoral behavior. Unfortunately, there are more similarities than differences between men of all races when it comes to how they treat women. More important, the majority of patrons, clients, or exploiters of this situation in developing countries where sex and romance tourism is rampant are white European males, which introduces a subject I will be exploring in a forthcoming book.

But since it's sisters who are dying and having their lives put at risk in alarming numbers, I have chosen to deal with the brothers on this one.

I also resist the temptation of framing it in a one-dimensional manner. Are these "good men"? Of the majority I would say, absolutely yes. Are they engaging in abusive behavior, and should they have an opportunity to correct it and be responsible? Absolutely!

For me, the more fundamental question is not whether we will hold men accountable, but when we will hold institutions accountable to men. If we raise girls and love boys, what does that mean given that we live in a society where being prepared is the only thing that really matters? I believe in men's capacity to change, but so much of that capacity rests on men's ability to unlearn certain behaviors, and a willingness to give up certain privileges—just at the time when they feel marginalized, stigmatized, or profiled. It is difficult to communicate what it means to be a black man. However, that does not mean one isn't held to a standard.

So when black men reject this—as I am sure some will—and when they get mad and say it doesn't apply to them because they haven't gone to Brazil or the Dominican Republic, that is cool, as long as they reject the behaviors as well. In other words, for these men to have a right to their indignation, they have to say not only that it does not apply, but also that it is wrong. By not coming out and saying, "That is wrong," they make it easy to distance themselves without taking a stance. In fact, they might be thinking, "That's not me, but I wish it was!"

To the black men who are married, we have to ask the question: Do you wish you could go? Given what I've said you should not be surprised about the number of these men who don't just want to go—they want to *move* to Brazil.

My goal as a black man is not to "out" my brothers. In fact, for the first time we have the opportunity to ask whether we can afford to act like white men. For so long, the black family and black men have been the proverbial scapegoat and whipping post for the larger mainstream white society. White men, being the pinnacle, have been the ones to emulate. Now for the first time, because of our economic and political gains, we have a unique opportunity to determine whether we will act like those who came before us. The face of the "ugly American" could very well be black now. Is that what blacks want?

Therefore, my goal is to gain some understanding and, hopefully, hold a mirror up for brothers to see how the black family structure is being wrecked, how the self-esteem of black sisters is being destroyed, and how black men are betraying our culture and legacy.

This book will be their wake-up call and, hopefully, an opportunity to build the heaven they are looking for right here in America, with their own women. Because it starts with black men.

If black men started honoring and respecting and treating black women like the queens that they are, they would have everything they're looking for right here. I have found that when a woman can truly trust her man, there isn't too much she wouldn't do for him. When her man makes her feel as though she is everything that she is, and that she can totally depend on him not to betray her and to work with her to build a life, there can be paradise.

I also want to give women hope. Not only are there brothers who treat women with respect and dignity, I also know there are men who want to change and are changing their current behavior. As a social worker, I have seen the changes in men who simply didn't know the ramifications of their actions, and when they got to see it, and see themselves, they changed.

In addition, I want to arm women with the tools to deal with the men in their lives and help them change. And if these men aren't willing to change, I want to help women learn how to weed these men out of their lives and move on.

I will give eight signs to know if your man is going to Brazil or elsewhere abroad. I will also provide comfort for women so that they will see that if their man is cheating on them—not just going to Brazil—it is not their fault.

Finally, revelation for some will come as no surprise. For some it will make logical sense that this is the behavior expected of men. To others, this will be the "last thing" black folks should have to deal with. Right when we are finally dealing with the immoral behavior of government officials, now we have to deal with *this*? What I would argue is that strength of the opposition is related to our ability to resist. In other words, if our "good men" are involved in these behaviors and are affected in these ways, one can reason that as a community we will not be in a position to truly resist the adversaries that are raised against us.

So this is not at all about individual or group pathology; it is about community accountability.

Chapter One

Eight Signs Your Man Is Traveling for Sex

Women always want to know, and they need to know, if their man is cheating on them. It is an age-old question. While I can't tell you if your man is cheating, I can give you some signs that will help you know whether he is heading to Brazil for sex.

The question isn't simply, "Is my man cheating?" But the real question should be, "Why?" I have attempted to answer that question.

And while many women are just in denial about their men, others are simply in the dark. Here is some light that might help you make some decisions about your man. Check out some of these signs:

1. He goes on trips for several days, often with a group of friends.

The first time I went down there I went with a large group of guys that I really didn't even know. Somebody put together

a trip, and there were twelve guys from my area—all broth-
ers. I was primarily with four other guys the entire time. We
were there five days on our first trip, and eight or nine on the
second trip.

It was eight hundred dollars for a ticket. If you do the
apartment together, it's no more than thirty to forty dollars a
night. The food is not expensive. Unless you're paying for a lot
of women, Brazil is not expensive at all. Everything is way
below the rate you would pay (in America). Going to Brazil
for eight days is cheaper than a weekend in Atlanta.

—Ralph, 43, IT manager, Myrtle Beach

The first part of this sign could be obvious, but if your man is going on a trip that lasts more than a week, and particularly if he is traveling with friends, he is more than likely going overseas to participate in a sex and romance vacation.

The average trip in Brazil, according to one of the top researchers of sexual tourism, is to Rio and is between seven and ten days. So this is not just "a night out with the boys." Rather, these extended vacations or "business" trips are about another kind of business.

And men are lying to get away. One of the men I interviewed, who had not made the trip but wanted to, told me, "I'm still trying to find a way to lie to get down there." Another black professional told his employer and colleagues that he was going on a missionary trip. That wasn't exactly a lie, because he did use the missionary position on at least one occasion. And he did scream out the Lord's name a couple of times.

2. His sexual appetite changes.

At twenty-five, I was still a novice at sex. Even though I was having sex for years, the biggest thing for me was numbers—how many women could I bang. As I got older, my concept of sex changed and I dealt more with pleasure and experiences. My fantasies changed. The more money you have, the more you go up your sexual scale. After you had a pretty woman, then a white woman, then an Asian woman, then two women together in Brazil, everything changes. With a black woman, you have to convince them that it's okay—that it will be confidential. I think that black women can be freaky. But they're not like the women in Brazil. You come back from Brazil knowing what you enjoy sexually.

A lot of black men that go there and come back start to expect something different sexually. If anything, my libido has increased. I might not have the physical prowess, but certainly I am stimulated to have sex at least once a day.

—Bill, 48, claims adjustor, Norfolk

This is perhaps the biggest one. On these trips, men don't just have sex; they also live out their sexual fantasies. As one man said matter-of-factly, "Everything you've seen on a video, I have done!"

What typically happens at first is that men just have rampant sex. However, on their subsequent trips they usually have made plans to do all the different things that they have only dreamed about or seen on videos. I talked with one man who was going for his second time, and I asked him what some of his expectations were for his upcoming trip.

He said, "This time I want to do a threesome, but with anal."

Invariably, this type of sexual adventurism leads them to have more varied sexual appetites and interests. A number of men come back from these trips going on about how sexually free Brazilian women are compared to their current or past partners.

3. His patience gets short.

Brazil gave me the confidence to leave a bad marriage.

—*Todd, 34, tax accountant, Boston*

Most of the men I interviewed talked about how these trips have been seminal events in their lives. They say things like "It was the best six days of my life" or "It was the greatest four days I have ever lived."

As a result, all the men talked about being changed in some way. One attorney told me, "You are really different when you come back. I can't explain it."

Often these men say that when they come back, they are not willing to put up with the same things that they did before. In their minds, they have a clearer idea of how a man should be treated, and they feel as though they should not have anything less.

One man told me, "It's hard to go from being the one chased to the traditional role of being the chaser. Once you have that experience of being treated like that, man, it's hard."

The end result is that many men come back with standards

for their relationships that make them less willing to put up with what they think is nonsense from their significant other. In the back of their minds they have other choices. This is how one brother explained it to me: "After I went to Brazil, I knew I had options."

It is precisely because of these trips that brothers get a little more impatient and also a little cockier about themselves, because they know—or think—they have a trump card.

4. He suddenly has more friends than he used to.

The guys down there introduced themselves to each other. I met a couple of brothers [in Brazil] who I still talk to—some guys from Nebraska, some guys from Minnesota. I think because of the way we met each other there's a special bond. You're walking toward a brother and you don't know each other and it's nothing to say, "What's up?" Back in the States on the streets, the one who says, "What's up?" first is usually the weaker one. The one who says, "What's up?" first is probably afraid. Here, you meet a guy on the first day, run into him again on the third whole day, and you're telling him all of the fun stuff you did. You start telling him where you hang out and the women he needs to call. You've got an instant network, so much so that I'm going to go on my fifth trip down there, and I ended up on a plane with a brother I met on the first trip. A guy I didn't even know.

This brother lives in Atlanta, and I can still call him and talk to him, find out what's going on out in Atlanta. It's just like that. I did my best networking when I was in Brazil.

—Tank, 37, hospital salesman, Oakland

If your man suddenly starts to have a more active group of friends than he did before, and it's not connected to his job, then you may want to watch him more closely. This increase of friends tends to coincide with one of these trips. This is consistent with how the men I've talked to describe expanding their social networks and groups of friends while they were in Brazil.

A Florida entrepreneur said, "It was the best networking that I have ever done."

What happens in Brazil is that men become part of a community, and they have these experiences that only they can talk with each other about. Why? Because other brothers don't get it. Men develop friendships and often exchange numbers and, at times, travel back to Brazil with men they met there.

So your man or husband may start to have new male friends in Atlanta or Los Angeles when you live in New York or Philly. You may begin to wonder how he knows all these guys. The other thing that might happen is that he may start to have friends in other countries. Typically, these professional black men talk about meeting and hanging out with men from Europe, Australia, and South Africa. They may even be white men. Unlike in America, they can actually be viewed and treated as equals, so these black men take some pride in keeping these relationships.

5. He has a lot more inside jokes and dropped calls when talking with friends.

Here's why it has been such a secret. Most guys won't just pick up and go; they have to be mentored. Somebody that's already been there has to take them. They say, "Come go; come go with me to Rio," and kind of show them the ropes. That's what happened to me. My frat brother took me.

—Jimmy, 28, semipro athlete, Pittsburgh

When you walk in the room and he's either talking on the phone or hanging with his friends and the conversation stops or abruptly switches, know that your man is up to something. If you start to feel that there is a lot more being said between him and his friends that you just don't get, start to question him. Or if he gets calls, but because he is with you he can't take the call, then you know.

The mistake that sisters might make is in thinking that these are other women he is trying to hide, which is exactly how he is able to be manipulative or tricky. The fact is, these are not his girls but his *boys*, calling to help plan, plot, or just reminisce about the experience they had abroad.

If I had a dime for every time a brother told me he was with his girl and couldn't talk, I would be a rich man. There is a lot both to share and to hide about these trips. In other words, men want to talk to other men and share with other men what they do, but they don't want to share it with women. So this creates an interesting dynamic of men sharing things in the presence of other people who just don't know.

A woman I interviewed said that a neighbor used a veiled threat against her that confused her. He said, "I see I better take your husband to Brazil." She had no clue what that meant. She will now.

6. He suddenly starts learning or speaking another language.

Brothers have to learn how to communicate in Brazil. Most don't venture off Copacabana. Brothers have been there three or four times and have never seen Sugarloaf Mountain or the statue of Christ. The only way they know how to communicate is with money, and when their money runs out, they can't communicate.

They don't understand that the more adventurous you get, the better it is. You have to learn the language. Just like the sisters here don't want us going to Rio, the sisters on Copacabana don't want us going to Villa Mimosa. The girls at Villa Mimosa don't want us going up into the upper country, to Queen Victoria. There are beautiful women in Queen Victoria. If you learn how to speak Portuguese, you don't have to pay for pussy!

—*Phillip, 45, graphic designer, St. Louis*

This may sound weird, but if he is trying to learn Portuguese, chances are he is (a) trying to get letters translated that the women he has met are sending him or (b) going through a transition where he is getting more interested in Brazilian culture.

7. He spends way more time on the Internet than he used to.

We send pictures and keep in contact all the time. Guys are always sending me e-mails and pictures. You've got to understand that for so long, we never had many options. And all of the sudden, boom! You've got the whole world open to you. You go there, and any woman you see, you can have.

—Sam, 32, counselor, Newark, New Jersey

The thing about Brazil is, if he is not there physically, he is often there virtually. The Internet and particularly the chat rooms about Brazil are huge, and they become one of the primary ways for men to talk about women and share stories in anonymity. Again, the interesting thing about this phenomenon is that it requires both confidentiality and collectivity.

In other words, men have to do this in ways that promote their anonymity and confidentiality, but at the same time, they want and need to share their stories. Remember, poor black men can't afford to know about this, and black women are not allowed to know about it. So the Internet and specifically the chat rooms become one of the primary tools that men use to stay constantly connected. In addition, the pictures and even the X-rated Brazilian porn are easily accessible online, and there are the sites such as Latin Europe, which has literally thousands of women wanting to come to America.

8. He has problems with your looks.

Halle Berry would be average in Brazil, very average. Sisters in America can't compete with that. How do I say this? When I come back to Ohio and I land in the airport, and I know it's so cruel to say it but the black women just all look fat and ugly to me. I hate to say this, but there are some women—professional and nonprofessional—who will let themselves go. They have children as they've gotten older; they're not in the gym; they're not concerned about working out; they don't necessarily keep their hair and stuff up to par, where if you want to compare that to the Brazilian women, not all of them, but the ones that people have interacted with in that Copacabana triangle in that area, they're working out. They already had the natural wavy hair. They got the green eyes because of the melting pot of people there. They are fine.

—Michael, 36, operations manager, Cleveland

Much of this whole phenomenon is founded on the belief and idea that Brazilian women are the most beautiful women in the world. Invariably, professional black men come back with problems with the way black women look. But it's deeper than the physical looks, although that's the driving force. The way Brazilian women look and care for themselves make black men see other things in black women that they feel are lacking. The comparison becomes very strong. And the mind-set is, why sift through the large number of black women to find one who works out and looks good and isn't overbearing, when you can have a sea of "perfect" women in Brazil?

So if your man starts making frequent disparaging comments about your looks and starts to be uninterested in you physically, he more than likely is comparing you to someone else.

Chapter Two

"How My Dick Spent the Summer": Getting Their Groove Back

Guys talk about Brazil, and they talk about the Dominican Republic and the Philippines. Those are like training wheels for travel. It's like a starter kit. The Greek Isles, the South of France—that's where it's happening. It just costs a fortune. I go to destinations that are affordable, like Indochina, Vietnam, Thailand, Cambodia. These places are very nice, very picturesque, and affordable. But I love Europe, Greece, France, and Hong Kong is off the hook, just very expensive.

There are a whole bunch of guys who are globetrotters. Those brothers have a lot of cash, and they are always on a plane going someplace. There are also dudes who run to Rio and to Bangkok. They can go to Bangkok or to Rio for the price of some rims. It's not just a guy with money who's doing this. For five or six hundred dollars, you can have a nice time in Brazil. The truth is that a ticket to Cleveland is more expen-

sive than a ticket to Rio. And the hotels in Cleveland may cost even more than a hotel in Rio.

All I'm saying is that if you can go visit your mama in Georgia, you can probably travel internationally. Maybe people are too poor to go visit their mama in Georgia, but if they can, they probably can go to Rio.

—David, 50, manager at a major chain, Chicago

Since day one, being a man of means has meant having sexual conquests—not just with women who look like you but all women. (From Solomon to now.) It's not enough to have sex with beautiful women in Miami; you have to have sex with beautiful women in Thailand. And if they have beautiful women in Iceland, you will go there, too. In general, men of means have been doing this for two thousand years. And today, African-American men do it because they can. For a little bit of extra money you can get on a plane and do that. For a week, ten days, or two weeks, you can experience the power that men of means experience every day. For some people, that week is like a lifetime.

—Jordan, 40, public relations, New York

My little clique, we do that. We get around. We've been to the Caribbean, to Colombia, and obviously to Brazil, to the Dominican Republic. There is talk now of [us going to] Southeast Asia. We live in a big city with a big airport, which is extremely international. Northwest has a relationship with KLM, so brothers can go to the Netherlands for six to seven

*hundred dollars. You get there, and marijuana is legal and
white women love you.*

—Mark, 42, systems analyst, Detroit

There is a scene in *How Stella Got Her Groove
Back* when Stella meets Winston's parents and
the mother asked Stella something to the effect, "Are things so bad in America that black women have
to travel overseas to find a man?" Although there has been
no movie made about black men who travel overseas to get
their groove back, one can imagine a similar scene where an
African-American man is asked, "Are things so bad in
America that black men have to travel overseas to find other
women?" Or depending on your perspective, the question
could be, "Are things so good in America that black men can
travel overseas to find other women?"

On one hand, black men have a long history of traveling
overseas—a point that is not missed by David, who has been
traveling to Brazil for more than two decades.

"Black men have been traveling the world since the twenties," he said. "There were big exoduses of black men during
the twenties and thirties to Paris because they were treated
better. Blacks were traveling when they were broke jazzmen
and they didn't have any money."

In this sense, David doesn't see the history of black men
traveling to Brazil as being any different from the history of
black men traveling to other foreign destinations. On the

other hand, the black men who travel overseas today have a much different context. David does notice a difference in the black men who travel to Brazil today:

> *I really hate to use the word "elite." They probably weren't broke; they seemed to be a little more knowledgeable class of people, people interested in seeing the world, people interested in world travel. As you know for yourself, the majority of people are born on their dot on this planet and don't leave it. Look at our president, George Bush. He never left the country until he became president, and he certainly had the means, but he wasn't interested in seeing the rest of the world. Here he was, a multimillionaire, and had never left the United States. So it isn't an issue of money; it's an issue of interest. Today you have a bunch of brothers dressed like thugs running around Brazil. I can't tell if they are professional or not.*

According to David, the early black travelers to Brazil were more like explorers. They were seeking not just sexual frontiers but social frontiers. David wasn't alone in his assessment of the early black travelers to Brazil. However, over time this class of black men who traveled to Brazil and other places has changed. Today's men are a part of a newer group of middle-class and professional black men who have unprecedented access to resources and income. Consequently, the black men who travel to Brazil today aren't like the group of artists and intellectuals who traveled to France in the 1920s and 1930s, or the jazz musicians who traveled throughout Europe during the '50s, or the political exiles or expatriates who traveled to places like Ghana and Tanzania during the '60s and '70s.

Unlike the black expatriates of the past, the black men who travel overseas today are more what the literature on sex tourism refers to as *sexpatriates,* or, in the case of Brazil, *mongers.* They are a part of an elite group of men who travel around the world for R & R, and while they are on their vacations they participate in what is referred to as I & I—intercourse and intoxication. Others go specifically for the three Fs: Find them, Fuck them, Forget them.

The Real Globetrotters or the New OGs

If David was an OG (original globetrotter) then, he differs markedly from the new class of black men or the new OGs who travel overseas to destinations like Brazil and participate in some form of sex tourism. Aside from social or intellectual interests, the big difference between black men twenty or thirty years ago was their income. In 2005 the median earnings for black males with a bachelor's degree or better was $44,675. To put it in perspective, in 1964 9.4 percent of blacks held professional or managerial positions, whereas in 1997 20 percent of employed African-Americans held professional or managerial jobs.

Middle-class and professional black men are aware of their class status as explained by Ralph:

This is why [travel to Brazil has] become more prevalent— because brothers are starting to make a lot more money, be-

cause they're allowing us to have positions. We're able to go to school and get these good jobs, becoming professionals, doctors, attorneys—higher positions in business, and sales positions that make a good bit of money. I remember back in the seventies, if you made twenty thousand a year, you were doing well. Now everybody makes at least twenty thousand.

Not only Ralph knows it; there is enough recognition of the economic prowess of black men that services are developed to cater to this new group. Astute businesspeople know that the most recent data provided by International Travel Association, shows that the vast majority of individuals who travel outside the United States come from two white-collar occupational categories: professional/technical (38 percent) and managerial/executive (27 percent).

So approximately 65 percent of people who travel outside the United States come from the two highest economic categories. In comparison, 5 percent are in clerical/sales, and only 2 percent are from the craftsman/factory worker category. In addition, the median income for people who travel outside the United States puts them in the top 10 percent nationwide.

Astute businesspeople also know that you can have flights to Rio de Janeiro from virtually anywhere in the United States, with nonstop flights originating from Houston, Miami, and Atlanta. From New York, Dallas, Washington, Los Angeles, San Francisco, and most of the rest of the country, you have to make a stop in Miami or in São Paolo to get to Rio. Consequently, new services are being aimed specifically at middle-class and professional black men to meet their travel needs.

Besides the more established sex tourist message boards like World Sex Tour Guide, the International Sex Guide, and Vikings Exotic Resorts, you can now find tourism agencies that cater specifically to black men. One such agency has a Web site that starts off with "From a black man's perspective, for the traveling man with an eye for exotic beauty." It then goes on to describe itself:

> *This site is dedicated to discussion about beautiful, sexy women in Brazil, specifically Rio de Janeiro and Salvador da Bahia in Brazil and other exotic locations through the world (Dominican Republic, Cuba, Malaysia, etc.). The goal of members is to conversate, meet, and travel in search of phat asses, sexy women, with safety and protection. Most, if not all, information is from a black man's point of view!!*

Like most good services, it even has a "Frequently Asked Questions" section, and one of the questions it addresses is, "Does the Club Only Travel to Brazil?"

> *The club travels to different places in the world (cities in Africa, Caribbean Islands, South America, Asia and the Philippines). Over 20 destinations. All the reports are on destinations where men are king and everything goes! Brazil is just one of the more favorite places the members like to go!* [edited]

This highlights two important aspects about black men's experiences overseas. First, men who participate in sexual tourism might have their favorite places to frequent, but they are increasingly traveling all over the world to have these experiences with women. It might be Brazil today, the Dominican Republic tomorrow, but as long as black men are looking for places where they can experience R & R or I & I and be exposed to an experience that only a select group of men in the world will have access to, then the place does not matter. This is how another man described it:

> It's not just Brazil. We'll find other places. There's Belize, Colombia, Venezuela—it's any Third World country, thanks to the revolutionary monetary system. This couldn't be done before we had the cashless society. We couldn't travel and stay for extended periods of time in other countries, because of the money-exchange issues. You could go for a little while, but you had to come back because you really couldn't access your money. But now, with debit cards, direct deposit, ATMs, credit cards, you can access your money anywhere in the world. I can be anywhere in the world and access every penny I've got. So now I don't need to be in America for the money now. Before, you had to be mega wealthy in order to be able to travel and live in another country. But now brothers are traveling and going everywhere.

As in the Calgon commercial, "Calgon, take me away!" there will always be places for men to go as long as there is a space in their mind that they can't get what they want here in the States and from black women. As long as they have the financial resources that allow it to happen, they will go.

Middle-income and professional black men are moving to more commercial and corporate ideas of social and intimate relationships between men and women. Commodified sexual relationships, or McSex, is just an efficient way of calculating risk and rewards in relationships. This is how one man explained it: "The thing [in Rio] is that everything is negotiation, everything is buy and sell. You realize when you come back from Brazil that it's not worth it. You may take a girl out to a nice restaurant, spend two fifty to three hundred dollars, and you're paying for a woman's time to see if you like her. And you spent that money only to find that you don't like her and she may not like you. You come back from Brazil and realize basically that there's inequity here. I shouldn't have to pay to see if I even like a woman."

He went on to say that this type of recognition allows him to see how all women fit in this way of interacting:

> *They're all programs. It's just the level at which the exchange is made. You have to realize the dynamic of it, which is that it's always going to be about the money in terms of whether a woman looks at you as somebody to marry. It's the same way over in Rio. It's all about the money. The only thing about it is, they've got fewer options for money, and money is relative. And you have more options.*

For the new class of black professional men, having access to all varieties of women comes with the benefits package, just like a salary and vacation time. The benefits are a set of expectations and entitlements to resources that separate them from other classes of men.

No Ordinary Johns: Sex Tourism

Men who pay for sex from prostitutes, so-called johns or tricks, are nothing new. Prostitution has been referred to as the world's oldest profession. Men who pay for prostitutes in the United States are from all backgrounds. Current estimates suggest that between 15 and 29 percent of all men have paid for sex with a prostitute. There are very few differences, in terms of age, education, and race, between the types of men who pay for sex.

Surprisingly, there are no huge income-based differences in the numbers of men who report having had sex with a prostitute. In fact, men in the bottom economic brackets report nearly identical rates of paying for sex as men in the top two economic brackets (33.4 percent versus 32.6 percent).

This is not the case for the category of men who participate in sexual or romance tourism. People who even have the ability to travel outside of the United States are a small group. So while overseas travel and tourism is an activity of the elite in general, overseas sexual tourism is the activity of elite men. In an article titled "How My Dick Spent Its Summer Vacation," authors Bishop and Robinson describe how sexual tourism in Thailand has become central to the Thai economy. They demonstrate how tourism—which is the world's largest industry—has become inextricably linked with national economies. They note, for example, that more than 70 percent of men who travel to Thailand are men traveling on their own, essentially to participate in the "economic miracle." But it is not just in Thailand. Look at some of the top Web sites to see that men travel all over the world for sex. You can even find listings for the twenty best destinations for sex tourism, which include the best brothels, massage parlors, go-go bars, and so on—all with detailed summaries and anecdotes from men who talk about their sexual experiences overseas.

So whether it is Thailand, Cambodia, Taiwan, South Korea, Vietnam, the Philippines, Cuba (which is fast becoming considered the Thailand of the Caribbean), Jamaica, Brazil, the Dominican Republic, or the Netherlands, men from all over the world travel to other shores and participate in "informal economies." What you find is that men travel to different places for different reasons.

Studies show that white Western men have been traveling to Third World countries to get access to exotic and erotic women for a long time. However, there tend to be certain niches where distinct national groups like to go. So just as African-Americans do not travel to the same destinations as white Americans in general, the same is true for black men who travel and participate in sex and romance tourism.

No Ordinary Sex Tourists: Mongers

Black American men typically travel to different locations compared to white Americans or European whites. They tend to travel in groups, whereas whites are more likely to travel alone. And black men tend to have different rationalizations and justifications for why they travel. Men who emerge from their experiences and exposures to the Brazilian sex scene can be categorized into three groups: rookies, veterans, and hard core. They are distinguished primarily by (a) the frequency of trips they take and (b) their relationship to the country and its women.

What these differences typically convey is a process that men go through as they establish more contact with the country and become more disconnected from America and black women. In general, men go from having rampant sex (*fantasy*) to having steady relationships with fewer women (*fantasy* + *relationship*) to developing more interest in the country. This interest can range from cultural to religious to financial interests, with some men ultimately moving to Brazil (*rupture with the past*).

Rookies are the men who have made the trip only a couple of times. They are considered rookies because they have limited exposure to the country, and their experience with Brazilian women is also very limited. Typically, these men have not gone outside the sex district. They have not participated in any of the usual tourist attractions. What distinguishes rookies from the other group of men is that their only relationship to the country is sex. Rookies have not moved away from black women . . . yet.

Veterans are the men who have traveled to Brazil a number of times and, as a result, know what to expect. They have talked with other men while they were there and have learned how to negotiate their experiences. These men talk of this as being "more familiar" with their circumstances. They know the better prostitutes. They know what areas are safer than others. They know the informal rules between customers and prostitutes. Perhaps more than anything, they have made the transition that allows them to have more of an individual experience in the country. This starts with no longer staying in hotels during their trips. Usually, beginning with their second trip, men start to rent apartments. This leads to the veterans living out more of their individual sexual fantasies. And while they are in the States they spend a lot of time involved in chat rooms and forums on the Internet that share information and provide updates about what is going on in Brazil. Veterans are beginning to move away from black women and are developing more sophisticated justifications for their behaviors.

Hardcore are the men who not only go regularly but typically have an investment in the country and with the women. Not only will they have a regular girl or girls, they may also have made overtures into investments either in businesses or in property. They have started to learn the language. They may even have traveled outside Rio to other parts of the country, and they more than likely have gotten into the cultural, religious, and sociohistorical aspects of Brazil. They know about the history and can talk about the African connection to Brazil. Some hard-core men have moved to Brazil, while others have married Brazilian women. In many cases this represents a sort of rupture with the past. These men have not just moved away from black women; by and large they are *anti*–black women.

Conclusion: Getting Their Groove Back

Just as Stella in Terry McMillan's novel was not the average black woman looking to get her groove back but rather an educated, successful black woman dealing with the challenges of being in relationships with professional black men, black men who travel to Brazil are not the average brothers looking to get their groove back, either. They are middle-income or high-income professional black men who, unlike Stella, are not traveling overseas because there are not comparable professional black women here in the States. Rather, they are traveling overseas for exactly the opposite reasons.

First, they are traveling because they have the financial means to do so. Second, they are traveling not only because of what they can't find in the States. So, unlike Stella, who appeared just to get lucky, men who travel to Third World locations may not have the intent to participate in sex tourism, but because of what is available to them, they know they always have the option. Finally, the reason why they go back is because the experience is so overwhelming that there is no comparison—a sentiment communicated by David:

I have been with hookers all over the world. The girls who work in Rio and in Europe, I have met hookers who are smarter than an MBA. They speak three and four languages and they know what's going on in Darfur and Chechnya. They can talk about international politics. They are very, very good at what they do and they make guys feel like they are in love with them. When you're with them, you aren't just buying a hooker, you're buying an experience.

It is the experience that men have on these trips overseas that makes it the phenomenon that it is. This phenomenon just can't be measured in terms of the number of men who go. If you ask a professional black man directly how big a phenomenon it is for black men to go on these trips, I'm sure he'll say a lot.

What these men end up trying to communicate is that there is simply no other place in the world today where African-American men voluntarily go in large numbers. As the same computer programmer from Orlando said, "When I was in Brazil, I ended up running into some of the brothers from my area. How the hell do you go outside the country and see people from your same area?"

Perhaps a more important question is, how many professional black men know about Brazil? And what does that mean to the minds and imaginations of other black men? Most men are very willing to share about their experiences in Brazil— under the right conditions, of course—to other men. Many, in fact, are adamant about telling other professional black men about Brazil. Some even sound as if it were their obligation to tell other men. As one man told me, "Every brother I see, I tell about Brazil. And I tell him he should go to know how it feels to be treated as a man."

Based on the number of men I have talked to who either have gone or know of other men who have gone, it challenges the concept of "six degrees of separation." In the case of professional black men, it appears to be more like "three degrees of separation," where at least one of every three professional black men knows someone personally who has gone to Brazil, has heard of someone who has gone, or has gone himself.

How many black men have physically gone does not reflect the large number of black men who have been exposed to, or influenced by, this phenomenon. Just think of the small number of men who play in the NBA. Now, compare that small number to the huge impact the NBA has on the imaginations of boys and men. The experience that men have in Brazil has that kind of reach among men and extends way beyond the numbers of men who have actually gone.

So the phenomenon can't be measured just in terms of the numbers of men who have gone—which are not small by any stretch of the imagination. And by most estimates, the number of men who do actually go continues to grow by leaps and bounds each year.

The final impact is on the family. Not all the men traveling abroad are single. The issue of black men and infidelity is nothing new. Tupac rapped about it in "I Get Around." Naughty by Nature's "OPP" talked about other people's property. And, of course, crooner R. Kelly sang about keeping it "On the Down Low." However, for a new class of black men who travel around the world with access to all these women, perhaps a new Terry McMillan book could be called *How Marcus Got His Groove Back.*

Chapter Three

"Just Drinking and Sexing": Hip-Hop and Middle-Class Masculinity

We all go out and sit in this restaurant and then suddenly there are all of these women. We hadn't been there three hours and there's a restaurant called Mia Pataca where everybody gathered. We're sitting there and it's almost like being in a VIP area. It's closed off. The only women they let come in are women that they think you might want to talk to. And all of a sudden, you're the object of what you think is a lot of people's desire, because everywhere you look, there's a woman trying to make eye contact with you.

Imagine that you and I are sitting outside a café and just across from you are thirty to forty women standing, waiting to be chosen. And these women are all tens and twelves, gorgeous. Perfect. Eventually, my boy and me grab this mulatto and this jet-black African.

We took them to what they called the "freak rooms." When we were done, I asked my boy if he wanted to switch. So I hit the mulatto and my boy hit the other chick. After that, we went back to Mia Pataca, and the plan was to go back to the hotel to rest, but some of the other guys wanted to go to this place called Quatro y Quatro.

The one guy that had been before kept talking about it. He said we should go at night because the best girls worked at night. Although we knew it was going to be a while before the club opened, we were so geeked we decided to go then.

Man, nothing he told us prepared me for what that place was like. You walk in and shit! They hand you a towel, a bar of soap, some flip-flops, and a robe. Man, I'm wearing a robe! Oh, and they give you a band and a locker to keep your shit in.

So we do all that and we go to the floor where the girls are. Oh, my God! Man, this dude said that the fine women worked at night, but he had to be lying, because I swear the finest women I had ever seen were there. I felt like I was in an Usher video. They were playing hip-hop, my boys and me were drinking, fine women everywhere. I was in heaven!

So while my boys were drinking and looking, I went and got a girl right away and took her up to the room. Man, I fucked the shit out of that girl. After that, I went back to the floor and they told me that my boy was already in the room, but with two women. I'm thinking, "Hell, no!" After I get a couple of drinks, I grabbed two women and took them back to the room. How many is that? Four or five by now, right? And we haven't been there a full night yet.

We get back to the hotel to rest, get some food, and whatnot. By the time we get there I was like, "Help!" I thought I was done.

The first time I walked into the hotel, I felt like the way attractive women must feel. I mean, there are all of these women that have that look—like they are going to strip out of their clothes right there. And you walk in and you're outnumbered by three or four as it is. And the women are so brazen. They just walk up to you and grab your hand.

I'm getting all of this attention—a lot more than I'm used to getting. And I'm not having to shell out all of that attention or put on that face to get it. You know how it felt? I felt like a ball player. I see why those guys do what they do. It's like a drug.

I'm in there and I realized quickly that I could just pick and choose. I'm brushing them off and I'm getting comments like "I'm looking at you," and "Hey, you. Turn around!" and "I'm sizing you up." I realized that I could have whatever I want. I knew some of them were in there working. But there were some who were legitimate, who just wanted to be out.

—Marcus, 28, marketing executive, Chicago

It's easier to imagine a group of inner-city boys running a train on a girl than it is to picture a group of *middle-class* boys running a train on a girl. Not only because of the stereotypical images portrayed in the popular media, or because of what has been painfully written about by writers like Nathan McCall, who courageously disclosed the perils of his inner-city upbringing in *Makes Me Wanna Holler*.

But there are also deep and unexamined ideas about sex and social class. We live in a society where the lower class is widely assumed to have more sexual prowess and to participate in a different type of sexuality than the middle and upper classes. This is especially true for African-Americans, where the black poor are often associated with a type of "dirty, funky sex" that allegedly Cornell West describes. And they are assigned to an entirely different category of sexuality from most Americans.

That is part of the reason why it is even harder to imagine a group of middle-class professional black men running a train on a woman, and yet this is the sort of thing that can occur when groups of professional men—lawyers, doctors, business executives—travel overseas to participate in sexual tourism. So while Marcus may be unusual in the amount of sex he had on his first day, he and his buddies are far from alone in their experiences of rampant or group sex while on vacation.

Marcus's situation is compelling precisely because it hints at some of these paradoxes. Marcus is what you would call the consummate rookie. He is a graduate of an HBCU and has never been married. When I first interviewed him, he recalled hearing about brothers going to Brazil as early as when he was in undergraduate school. In fact, he heard that brothers made trips to Brazil as graduation gifts to themselves. He said jokingly, "As business majors, we always find ways to pay for things."

By the time I had talked with him, he had gone to Brazil three times in one year alone. And was planning a fourth.

"I have to go back," he said. "I can't wait to go back again."

Ironically, Marcus never considered going to Brazil, let alone going as often as he does now. When guys—particularly his frat brothers—used to tell him about their trips and even went so far as to show pictures they had brought back, he would respond, "I ain't never bought pussy, so why would I go overseas and buy pussy?"

Before going to Brazil, Marcus was like many other young professional black men in that he was not necessarily against black women. But he was not necessarily committed to them, either. He said he had been in relationships with sisters in the past, some good and some bad. Marcus said that sisters were constantly attracted and available to him. Self-described as 6'1" and 205 pounds this former athlete said matter-of-factly, "I have never had a problem with sisters."

So when he initially decided to go to Brazil it was not because he had a difficult time in relationships with black women, but rather because he kept hearing about it more and more.

"Sure, I was dating at the time, but nothing serious," he said. "My frat brothers kept talking about how off the hook it was. I mean, they couldn't stop talking about it!"

These days, Marcus goes so often that he frequently expands the network of professional black men that he travels with. Most recently he met up with a group of lawyers there. The next trip he is planning is with a mixed group of professionals.

The obvious question is, how and why did Marcus go from never "paying for pussy" and not hanging out in strip clubs in the United States to becoming "King Ding-a-Ling" and participating in threesomes, double penetrations, and running trains on women? The answer can be found in Marcus's notion of taking off his "mask."

I didn't feel any problems from the guys who were down there, either. I didn't see any confrontations. You're talking about clubs full of black people and there were no confrontations. It was just good. I wasn't constantly watching my back. I wasn't on guard the whole time. There weren't brothers stepping on each other's feet. If they did, there wasn't a problem.

In fact, you might hear someone say, "Brother, let me get you another drink." I heard brothers say that so much down there. And I think it was kind of like what Richard Pryor said when he went to Africa and said he didn't see any niggers. That's what it felt like.

Was it a good night or what? It was a dream.

And the night wasn't over. When we back to the hotel, I picked out the one I wanted and we went back to the room. I must have been tired and drunk because I couldn't handle my business, so I took a Viagra. After that, I passed out. I woke up later to a knock at the door. When I opened it, there was this chick standing there naked saying some shit, waving, and telling me to come on. I followed her down the hall to my boy's room. He was in there with another girl, so I was like, "Fuck it!" I took another Viagra.

At this point, I'm doing everything but I can't bust a nut. I'm fucking in the ass, in the pussy. We're doing all types of shit, like double penetration, and I still can't cum. It was the weirdest thing. Before we started fucking, we're sitting there and one girl was looking at us and the other girl was compar-

*ing whose dick was bigger. We were actually sitting around
talking. I was very vulnerable, and I was thinking how I
would never expose myself like that back at home.*

*It was almost like the locker room. You're walking around
naked and there is that bonding and that vulnerability, but it
is not sexual. It's not like you're looking at your boy. You're not
looking at them like, "Oh, yeah, my boy's got his clothes off." It's
almost like "Here, the mask's off. This is me."*

The idea of wearing a mask is nothing new for black folks.
Essentially, it refers to how we create an outer shell for others and live behind it. Paul Lawrence Dunbar made the idea
famous in "We Wear the Mask":

> *We wear the mask that grins and lies,*
> *It hides our cheeks and shades our eyes . . .*

This 1913 poem laments how black people wear masks
to protect their inner lives from the assault of white racism.
Frantz Fanon popularized this sentiment in the 1960s in
"Black Skin, White Masks," by describing the psychological process that colonized people go through in confronting
their oppression. Richard Majors related the idea specifically
to black men in the 1990s by demonstrating how black men
often present an exterior, what he referred to as "cool pose," to
deflect any sense of vulnerability. However, unlike Dunbar's
mask of race, Fanon's mask of colonialism, or Major's mask
of the streets, the mask that Marcus described and that he
experienced as oppressive and denying access to his inner life

was a sexual mask. More important, unlike the other masks, Marcus's embrace of vulnerability enabled him to shed the mask.

To understand why Marcus and many other middle-class professional black men feel that they are able to unmask and reveal a part of who they are (at least sexually) overseas, one has to understand the relationship between sex and social class, and the influence of hip-hop on middle-class masculinity.

Brazil and Context

In many ways, listening to Marcus's story, it is easy to see the relationship between hip-hop and black men's experiences in Brazil. Rio offers access to two of the most dominant venues in hip-hop: the dance club and the strip club. In hip-hop lyrics and certainly in hip-hop videos, the dance club and the strip club are two primary stages where the public performance of hip-hop culture occurs, meaning these are the main places where people come together and where the styles (looks and clothes) and behaviors of hip-hop are on display. Rio, it just so happens, is known for taking those two elements to an entirely different level in the minds of professional black men.

Club Help, which Marcus referred to, is widely considered one of the biggest and best dance clubs in all Latin America. With reportedly the best deejays in the country, playing a mixture of hip-hop, samba, and salsa, the club is able to attract men and women from all over the city. It is well known that not only are the women in Club Help gorgeous (and they come in sexy attire), but also they outnumber men on crowded nights four to one. Add to that drinking and women dancing, and most men describe an almost surreal experience.

Club Help is also by far the most prolific destination for sex tourism in Rio. It is located in Copacabana and not far from the beach, hotels, and restaurants, including the best known, Mia Pataca. Consequently, it is a place that almost every professional man, black or white, has heard about or gone to. It is a place where you can talk to women, buy drinks, watch them dance, and also make a sexual connection should you desire to.

Termas, on the other hand, is best described as a combination strip club and brothel. By all accounts, Termas in Rio makes strip clubs in the United States look like Chuck E. Cheese. In strip clubs in the United States, the average man can expect to be rubbed up against and have some tits and ass shaken in his face. At the end of the night, he is left to his own devices to satisfy whatever sexual urges may have been stirred. In Termas, not only are men exposed to beautiful women who are there to dance and provoke their sexual urges, they are also there to satisfy each and every urge that is stirred.

That Marcus and other professional men are having rampant sex is not the same as having *random* sex. In fact, there is nothing random about their sexual experiences at all. Rather, there is a coherent logic and a set of meanings embedded in each sexual experience that mirror the type of sexuality expressed in hip-hop and rap. So while Club Help and Termas offer a context for black men's behavior, hip-hop provides the content of its meanings.

Hip-Hop and the Black Middle Class

When we talk about the impact of hip-hop on the black community, invariably we end up talking about one of two groups: black women and girls, or inner-city black males. Black women and girls are concerned about the derogatory lyrics and the overt sexism so often found in hip-hop videos. Their concern stems from statistics that show black women suffering from a disproportionate rate of physical and sexual abuse, and from research studies that link high exposure to hip-hop with female victimization.

For black males, the concern is often aimed at a culture of violence and hypermasculinity persistently communicated by hip-hop and rap lyrics and videos. The battery of statistics that demonstrate the high morbidity and mortality of black males, the high incarceration rates, and the low level of academic success often reflect a concern over hip-hop and its negative affects. A recent PBS documentary, "Beyond Beats and Rhymes," is indicative of the types of questions raised about the impact of hip-hop:

1. What is the relationship between masculinity and violence?
2. What role do sexism, misogyny, and homophobia play?
3. What role does the larger music industry play?

The problem with such an approach is that it potentially obscures an entire class of people who may be profoundly affected by hip-hop but who may not show up in the conventional statistics and who may not act in ways that appear overtly hypermasculine. Certainly this is the case for whites, but also for the black middle class. In fact, it is rare to hear any question about the impact of hip-hop on the black middle class.

Patillo McCoy's book *Black Picket Fences* offered one of the few examinations of a black middle-class neighborhood that looked directly at the impact of hip-hop culture on the black middle class. She found that many black middle-class youth are caught in a "ghetto trance," where the style and behavior associated with hip-hop shapes their everyday lives. Unfortunately, such rich studies are rare, and the focus is mainly on youth and young adults. What has never been really looked at is the impact of hip-hop on middle-class men. Hip-hop gives voice to certain black men while denying a voice to others. Consequently, black middle-class masculinity gets masked, making it invisible or irrelevant.

Hip-Hop and the Negation of Middle-Class Masculinity

There are a number of masculine themes communicated by hip-hop. Those related to images of materialism (the baller) and violence (the thug) are probably the most common. However, sexually another major dimension of masculinity is also communicated in hip-hop, so much so that the archetypal images of pimps and players are commonplace in today's culture. You can even catch a Nike commercial featuring LeBron James, in which one of his several personalities is either a pimp or a player—it's hard to tell the difference. The point is that these sexual images of black men are ubiquitous.

The real power of hip-hop lies in both its lyrical content and its visual cues and production. The lyrical content of hip-hop and rap provides a guide to a narrow type of masculinity, whereas the videos portray images of black men in relationship to black women and their bodies. It doesn't matter whether it is the Snoop and Ferrell video, which was reportedly done in Rio, or the Ludacris song "Pimpin' All over the World," which makes reference to Brazilian women—hip-hop helped shape and influence the experience of African-American men, especially younger middle-class men who travel to Brazil.

For the men who travel to Brazil, there are three crucial aspects about hip-hop masculinity that make their trips and experiences so powerful and memorable: compulsive heterosexuality, sexual potency and militancy, and pornographic public performance.

Hip-hop and rap are legendary for their compulsive heterosexuality. It's rare to hear a hip-hop or rap song that's *not* talking about sex. Either artists are yelling it loud:

> *(Oh, Oh, Oh) Girl give me that*
> *Girl give me that (pussy) . . .*
> — "Give Me That," Lil' Boosie & Webbie

Or they are whispering it:

> *Ay, bitch! Wait till you see my dick;*
> *Im'a beat dat pussy up . . .*
> — "The Whisper Song," Ying Yang Twins

In either case, the compulsive masculinity found in hip-hop typically portrays males as either always looking for "pussy" or never in a position to turn down pussy if it is presented to them. This is exactly what Marcus described. First, when he was at Terma, he was not to be outdone by his boys. He had to make sure he had another go-round—with two girls. The second time, when he awakened from his drunken stupor at the hotel, instead of saying, "I'm tired; I already have had sex with seven different women, and I'm a little drunk," he got up and continued his marathon course of sex. Not only did he have more sex, he also had to pop a pill to assist him. The use of performance-enhancing drugs is the greatest evidence of the type of compulsive and obligatory sexuality that often occurs on these trips. Otherwise healthy, normal, and virile men are reduced to taking buckets of Viagra, Levitra, and Cialis.

The important thing to understand about compulsive heterosexuality is that *performance* replaces desire. The typical image of a man taking sexual-enhancement pills is of an older man who has to do so because, while he has plenty of desire, his physical ability to perform has left him. Marcus, who is twenty-eight years old, is certainly physically able to perform. When he was participating in the orgiastic sex free-for-all, where he was having anal, vaginal, and anywhere-he-could-stick-his-penis sex, he had no problems initially getting an erection. It was not because he had a strong sexual desire but rather because he had a profound, almost obligatory desire to perform.

Marcus, and men like him, are compelled to have as much sex as they can, not because they start off as sexually insatiable but because with modern medicine they are physically capable. Therefore, if they cannot sustain that performance with a natural sex drive, they are all too open to taking sexual-enhancement pills to assist in their performance.

The ever-present theme of sexual potency in hip-hop is one of the primary ways to mask middle-class masculinity. The idea of sexual potency is best communicated by the famous words of the Notorious B.I.G. (a.k.a. Biggie Smalls), who said, "No lovemaking, just back breaking."

Contemporary hip-hop and rap are therefore largely about black men performing a potent form of sex and sexuality, which can be heard in lyrics like: "Im'a beat dat pussy up!" Whether it is the Ying Yang Twins' "Whisper Song" or 50 Cent's "Magic Stick," the message is all the same—there is nothing weak or ineffectual about black men's sexuality.

While the image of sexually potent black males is far from new, what makes black male sexual potency in hip-hop different from past expressions is the militancy and the related authenticity of blackness that occurs along with it. In other words, the image of black men's sexuality communicated by hip-hop doesn't rely solely on the white racist's imagination as it did in the past.

Historically, whites created the stereotypical images of sexually potent black men to keep African-Americans subordinate. But whites alone couldn't sustain this image. Blacks foster it. And they make it legitimate because, through hip-hop, they promote it. The message is, if you're a "real" black man, you're potent. Consequently, it is not at all uncommon to hear rap artists refer to their street credentials.

Ho', you don't know nann nigga, uh–uh
That'll represent like me . . .

One of the fundamental ways that hip-hop works is through constant attempts at authenticating blackness, and it does so by creating boundaries around sex and images of the streets. The consequence, of course, is that the main boundaries are among other black people, not whites. There can be no real value in telling white people that they are not black enough or "street" enough. Consequently, it is middle-class black men and boys who are denied access to this type of militant and potent form of sexuality—not just whites. Perhaps one of the most glaring examples of how hip-hop creates boundaries around sex and class that exclude middle-class black men is in its relationship to pornography.

Make no mistake about it, men watch pornography. Much of contemporary pornography, and especially black pornography, is deeply influenced by hip-hop. Hip-hop artists frequently make underground videos, while others like Snoop and Ice T have mainstream black porn. However, the real impact of hip-hop on black pornography isn't just the artists who sponsor and endorse it, or the music that often provides a background in it; it is the themes of sexual potency—particularly penis size and the streets that give meaning to it.

Look at the titles of some popular pornography tunes: "Parking Lot Pimpin'," "Pimpin Ain't Easy," "Pimp Juice," "Pimpformation," "She Got Pimped," "Homies and Ho's." Constant themes in hip-hop portray black men as hustlers, pimps, and players—all highlighting the sexual exploits of nonprofessional black men. The erasure of professional black men from the images of black men's sexuality in pornography wasn't lost on the researcher Gail Dines, who said,

> *Should the black man rise above the "hood" and enter the middle class, however, he would then cease to be an "authentic" black man and would thus be rendered invisible in IP. The middle class black man is missing from these movies because his class mobility and his allegiance to a more "educated" form of masculinity render him white.*

Consequently, in the world of pornography, it is not just that "all men are not created equal. They are not all equally endowed with 'enormous' and 'gigantic' penises by their 'creator.'" So for professional black men looking to find images or expressions of their racial and sexual identity in pornography, they will not see themselves. Like white men, they are reduced to spectators watching voyeuristically from the sidelines.

All porn watching, to some degree, is about watching other men perform, and the popular gonzo style of pornography only heightens that experience. When black professional men mention to me, as many tend to do, that they have done *everything* in Brazil that has been done on the porn videos, they are talking about reproducing what nonprofessional black men do.

Regrettably, this has not been the issue that researchers who work in the area of race and pornography have been most interested in exploring. There is an acknowledgment of how class differences among black men actually drive much of the imagery in porn, both black and white, where lower-class black men provide the most potent images of black sexuality. But the concern appears to be aimed more at addressing why white men consume such images, and the consequences, rather than what the implications are for middle-class black men who consume those same images. Presumably, there is a difference between a white man, of whatever class background, who looks at black men performing pornographic sex wondering or even wishing to be him, and a black man who is not from the street, seeing the same images. (Of course, the true irony is when a former professional such as Lexington Steele plays a street black person in a porn video.) What this leads to is the idea that whites should be the most concerned about how black people are portrayed in pornography.

Interestingly enough, the group that probably receives the least attention in race and pornography is professional black women. While lower-class black men take center stage as "fuckers" in pornography, it is often inner-city hood rats, bitches, and ho's who end up sharing the spotlight as "fuckees." Just as in rap videos, one rarely finds an image of a black woman with a job, let alone sees a middle-class professional black woman. This might be perceived as a positive in that professional black women are spared the type of coding that portrays them as dick-loving freaks who always want to fuck the way that poor or inner-city black women are perceived.

Instead, professional black women are to be treated like ladies. But this perception can also lead to the notion that professional black women do not have a sexuality—or, worse, that they are frigid. The absence and erasure of both professional black men and women from adult entertainment leaves unaddressed the question of what sex is like for this group.

Meanings and Interpretation

In the absence of any definitive answers to these questions, Brazil sets the stage for black men to go out and literally enact hip-hop masculinity and sexuality in ways that are influenced by the images that other black men provide. So when it comes to many of the experiences that black men have in Rio, social as well as sexual, hip-hop provides a primary way of establishing meaning and interpretation.

For Marcus, the power derived from the experience of being in Club Help is due in part to the fact that most adult men have been to a club in the past and know what it is like to desire a women in those settings. Therefore, most men can automatically plug into the experience of seeing attractive women whom they yearn to be with physically.

Consequently, when the club scenario is altered, flipped, as in Club Help, where the men become the subjects rather than the objects of desire, it becomes powerful, not just because it is new or because it reverses their historical roles. Where this experience draws its meaning, according to Marcus, is from the idea of what it means to be a "baller."

This is essentially a situation where individual men draw their personal experience from a social environment where women collectively desire them. Again, it would be enough to have just one beautiful woman who wanted him—what most men in the United States could only hope for in a club—but having many beautiful women desire him is what he attributes to being a "baller." The idea of being looked at and wanted and desired is the deep "hypnotic effect" that men talk about time and time again when speaking of their experiences abroad. Marcus likened his experience to being in the VIP section in a popular club.

When it comes to men's experiences at Termas, sex is not the only thing that they get. As Marcus described in the opening, men get a level of personal service that is unheard of in the States. If you can imagine the level of physical pampering that a woman receives when she goes to get a massage, a facial, and a pedicure at a spa, then you can understand what men like Marcus experience at Termas. Walking around in their bathrobes and slippers, black professional men are treated like the ultimate player or pimp. To be serviced by women sexually and to be catered to in the presence of other men, in a way that is safe and noncompetitive, is the ultimate experience.

The issue of safety was important for Marcus and other professional black men in all these experiences. Unlike in the United States, where brothers often have to watch their backs, Club Help is not associated with violence, and brothers don't have to compete for the attention of women. This is not a small thing, because even with all the frivolity in the social interaction in hip-hop, there is always a threat of violence where a fight can break out or someone can get shot "up in the club." In contrast, black men treat each other with a high degree of deference and respect in the clubs in Rio and during all of their social outing. The issue of safety is probably the most important issue in the sexual unmasking that Marcus and other middle-class black men experience in Brazil, because it is linked to vulnerability. The vulnerability he spoke of didn't have anything to do with the women; it had to do with other men. Unlike in hip-hop, where masculinity is competitive and judgmental, Marcus felt that he was in a safe space with other professional black men.

Although much of the sex was about performance, there was no anxiety attached to it. In fact, lack of anxiety leads to more intimacy, but the intimacy is with other black men. This speaks volumes to the need for recognition by other men that hip-hop masculinity breeds hostility.

In Brazil, American black men don't feel invisible sexually. The isolation of black professional men in the workforce creates a context for male bonding and friendship formation that is essential for the black men who go to Brazil. According to a leading researcher in Brazil, unlike white males who travel more by themselves, black men mainly travel in groups. Because so much of the experience of going to Brazil was about identifying with men, it was also about objectifying the Brazilian women. When Marcus referred to the notion that it was about what we did to the girl, he was explicitly saying that she was a sexual object whose feelings and thoughts did not matter as much as the affirmation and recognition of other men.

This also shows that hip-hop is not good at producing happiness. It is much better at manufacturing pleasure—as with its pornography—but that isn't the same thing as happiness. In fact, with the violence, the substance abuse, and the snarls, it is not clear if hip-hop and rap have anything to do with happiness, contentment, or fulfillment. Even when people seem to be having fun, there always appears to be a snarl somewhere beneath the smile.

In contrast, the professional black men visiting Brazil describe a level of happiness unlike anything they have ever experienced in the United States. The reason for this is that they can participate in "hoodlike" activities but not have the same hoodlike consequences. The brothers can go out to the club and not worry about getting shot or getting into fights. They can participate in a set of relationships where brothers treat each other with respect and regard. All these various themes and dimensions of hip-hop masculinity are what mediates the experiences of black men who travel to Brazil, whether in a strict social setting or in explicit sexual situations. As a result, Mia Pataca, Club Help, and Termas are the unfolding places for black male sexuality.

Conclusion

Hip-hop raises the question of who is having sex in black America and what is happening when they have sex. In terms of sex and social class, it suggests that nonprofessional black men have the most potency and prowess. Ironically, though, the research suggests that professional black men may be the true pimps and players.

The suggestion that hip-hop influences middle-class masculinity does not mean that professional black men travel to Brazil and somehow magically transform into or become NWA, or "niggers with attitudes." Nor is it that without being exposed to hip-hop these men would not follow a similar logic in terms of rampant sex. Rather, the argument is that without hip-hop these experiences would not have the same meaning.

For professional black men, especially younger men, hip-hop provides a template for giving meaning and interpretations to their experiences, both sexual and social. What Brazil does is offer access to the dominant images of ballers, players, and pimps through some of the key venues enshrined in hip-hop, such as the dance club and strip club.

The key to understanding why Brazil is so effective at providing men with these sexual experiences is not just the level of anonymity and confidentiality; it's the same idea that goes with "whatever happens in Vegas stays in Vegas." Most of these experiences, sexual and otherwise, are very public, but whatever happens in Brazil stays in Brazil.

Going to Rio is like walking into a rap video: scantily clad women, gyrating and fawning over every man in sight. What Rio does is provide a cover for middle-class men to remove their veil, their masks, and do things they only imagined. They get to live out their fantasies. They get to be the rappers in the rap videos. For them the feeling is potent, public, and militant.

The relationship between hip-hop and pornography becomes another very specific way that black professional men become visible. When they enact pornographic sex acts, such as double penetration, cumming on a woman's face, and so on, they are making themselves visible in the black pornographic imagination.

In spite of the many similarities between hip-hop masculinity and the sexual activities that black professional men do in Brazil, there are important differences. Professional black men may adopt hip-hop masculinity, but they adapt it to meet their class needs. That is why, unlike the men in hip-hip, it is important that professional black men treat each other with respect and regard.

The sexual mask that Marcus felt he was able to shed in Brazil comes with a cost. For him and others, it came at the cost of buying into things I have already covered: sexual performance separated from sexual desire, intercourse without intimacy, and all those other things we already know. But it also may have opened additional wounds. When Marcus talked about trying three and four partners, in some respects he was opening the floodgates for a type of addiction that many men experience as "sexual freedom" or "having different standards."

What that sexual freedom actually ended up masking was potentially an entire level of addiction, confused with high standards, that many men who have traveled to Brazil talk about. The sexual mask that men like Marcus thought they were able to shed also came at the expense of black women.

A Message to Black Women

Professional black women have always been at the forefront of arguing against the negative images propagated by hip-hop. Whether the late C. Delores Tucker, the black female students at Howard University who started the campaign to stop BET's pornographic *Uncut*, or the black women at Spelman College who organized against rapper Nelly's "Tip Drill" video—where he swipes a credit card between a black woman's buttocks—black women have always taken a stand. Invariably this has put them at odds with nonprofessional men who perpetuate these negative images.

Thus far, professional black men have been able to reap the benefits of consuming and participating in these negative images of black women without sharing the load of the criticism. This is because the middle class does not overtly demonstrate this behavior, and now that these men can go overseas and act out their hip-hop fantasies, it is even easier to be complicit in this behavior.

Chapter Four

"I Thought I Was Going to Die": Old Dirty Bastard or Middle-Age Masculinity

I don't want to say old men, but the older men like the girls that are twenty-one, twenty-two, twenty-three. But for the most part, those young girls aren't interested in us (in America). They think it's gross to be with an older man—that is, until he gives them money.

As a young man, I had a ton of options. But then I got married. While I was married I wasn't really looking for those types of options. I was just trying to build things for the family. When I turned forty I get divorced. Now, if you look at it, somewhere in their later thirties and early forties is when men begin to get divorced. People call it our midlife crisis. It's a midlife crisis when you are married and doing that—not when you are single.

We start looking at these same young girls that we liked before we got married, because we haven't really changed by being married. We were probably a little more faithful—at least I was. So now that I need a woman again, I began look-ing at these young girls. Well, the young girls weren't inter-ested, because I didn't have that kind of flavor. When I say that kind of flavor, I'm talking a million dollars plus.

If you hit the million-plus status, your options are infinite—from women your age all the way down to women in their twenties ... eighteen, if you're really crazy. At forty-eight, it's harder to go back and find an eighteen-year-old. You're looked at like you're a dirty old man if you're even going to a club where young people hang out. I'm telling you, I felt like a dirty old man because I've got daughters older than eighteen. I went to a club and I saw this girl that was in my daughter's class! I'm immediately thinking, "I've got to get out of here!"

But over in Rio it's no big deal. If I see a girl that's eigh-teen, she's not off limits. It's not even looked at. In Rio, I'm having a different girl every night. And usually every sexu-ally fantasy I ever had was fulfilled. On my last trip ... I got scared because I thought, "Lord, am I about to die? Because you've given me everything!"

Most of the time, brothers don't verbalize what their sex-ual fantasies are, you know. So, it was like the Lord knew what my sexual fantasies were because they were hidden in my heart.

—Morgan, 49, information technology manager, Detroit

They say variety is the spice of life. People grow up hearing that phrase. Men grow up hearing a slightly different version of it: "Nothing is better than pussy, except for *new* pussy." National sex surveys confirm that most men think about sex at least once a day. And yet, the image of a man who thinks about sex all the time is of a young man, typically around eighteen, who is at his peak sexually. It's not of a man in his thirties, and certainly not a man in his forties, fifties, or sixties.

Brazil explodes that image for adult men! What Brazil does for younger professional black men is to allow them to live out a sexual script that is typically lived out by men in the hip-hop set. For older professional black men, Brazil allows them to live out sexual fantasies, influenced by their sense of mortality, the realities of their changing bodies, and the reality of their careers (both good and bad). More important, Brazil offers older men the idea that their age is not a symbol of declining sexuality, or evidence of some deviant characteristic. Age and sexuality are embraced in Brazil and throughout Latin America. This is how David, a man in his late forties, talked about Brazil and Latin countries in general:

> *A dirty old man. What is that? In this country you get old quick because everything is so youth conscious. You go overseas, especially Latin countries, even places like Italy, Spain, and France, and old guys are considered sexy. Look at Spanish TV and see who the leads are on their soap operas—grayhaired dudes. Look at the Spanish soap operas and see who*

are the hunks—cats in their fifties and sixties. Older black guys go overseas, and all of sudden, young chicks are hitting on them . . .

This idea that older men are not allowed to express their sexuality in American society is something shared by many older African-American men. Bill, a black professional in his forties, said, "We didn't suddenly give up. It is society that gives up on us, and I don't think it is fair."

Consequently, Morgan is just one of the many black men over the age of forty who go to Brazil to live out a life they think has been taken away from them due to age and their restricted financial situation in the States. Brazil essentially allows him to regain his mojo—his sexual and financial vitality. In his particular case, it leads to the enactment of sexual fantasies, ideas of sexual grandeur, and often a preoccupation with young women.

The Freaks Come Out with Age

Most people tend to focus on the decline in the frequency of men's sexual activity with age. The usual story goes that after a man hits his sexual peak at age eighteen, he begins a precipitous decline that includes weaker erections, less forceful ejaculations, decrease in sex drive or libido, increased refractory time between ejaculations, and so on. So by the time a man reaches his forties and fifties, he can expect a dismal future with his sex life.

However, most people don't recognize that a man's sexual

variety actually increases with age. Virtually every major sex survey demonstrates that men get freakier sexually as they get older. The older he gets, the more a man's sexual repertoire increases. Men actually participate in a greater variety of sexual activities. On one hand, this might sound simple, given that as people get older they might be expected to experience or participate in different things, sexually and otherwise.

According to the most current survey on sex and sexuality today, heterosexual men now engage more in anal intercourse and oral sex, as well as more varied forms of sexual contact.

The research also shows that not only are men more likely to be involved in a greater variety of sexual activities as they age, they are also more likely to have affairs. In fact, men between the ages of forty and fifty-nine have a higher rate of infidelity than men in their twenties and thirties. So not only do older men have a greater variety of sexual activity and appetites, they tend to have sex with different people. In addition, men with more income have the highest rates of infidelity, and men with graduate degrees reported the highest rate of infidelity.

So given that age and income lead to greater sexual variety and greater rates of infidelity, the question becomes, what is driving this? Part of the answer is that older men disagree with the common belief that women hit their sexual prime as they get older. This is what Mark, another computer technology professional, had to say about the subject:

That's the biggest fallacy that has ever been fabricated. I laugh at that. When all of the brothers get together and talk away from our wives and are drinking and shooting pool, the first thing that comes out is that none of us is getting any. I know I ain't getting none. I will tell you the truth: women who are in their forties and fifties feel it is a necessity to be sexually active. It's a chore. In my opinion, I believe once they get you to sign that paper [marriage license] they feel like they can use their pussy as a bargaining tool for appliances, trips, you name it.

They were freaks before they got married. Even my own ex-wife gave me plenty of pussy before we got married. Then when we got married, it all changed. I have friends in my office, and they tell me the same thing. You see guys my age say that they don't want to necessarily fool around, so they go to the titty bar. I go to this shady neighborhood, get my fantasies met, and then rush back to my quiet, conservative suburb. Well in Rio there is no rushing . . .

Mark believes that sex becomes a bargaining chip for women as they get older and that marriage actually changes the dynamics of sex. In fact, he believes that this is something that younger guys don't have to deal with. According to Mark, "The younger guys have a whole different situation. Guys in their thirties, their women are a whole other generation altogether. Their women have no problem with oral sex or experimenting."

So there is a belief that as women get older they are less interested in sex and that this separates older men from younger men, not because they are different but because older women are different. However, like a lot of things with men, while the focus may start off being put on other people, the real issue influencing older men and their sexuality is their *own* aging process.

Men like Morgan and Mark, who are in their forties and early fifties, would not call themselves this, but they are essentially baby boomers—black baby boomers, to be more specific. They are a part of the estimated 9.1 million black boomers as of 2004. Morgan specifically is a part of the late boomer generation, born between 1956 and 1964. That age group, researchers show, is typically burdened with spending money on mortgages and children's tuition and putting money in their 401K for retirement. This generation is also referred to as the "sandwich generation"—sandwiched between their children and their parents. For many, it is a time for serious confrontation with life.

Confronting middle age comes with an entirely different set of challenges for black men. While midlife can be a terrifying experience for men in general who may sense the "second half of life," it can be particularly challenging for older black men who begin to see their life for what it really is.

One major issue is the changes in men's physical bodies, which are magnified because of issues specific to black men. General morbidity and chronic illnesses such as hypertension, diabetes, cardiovascular disease, and prostate cancer become significant factors in black men's lives as they age.

"It is scary," said Mark. "I remember going to the doctor not too long ago, and I remember thinking that this happens in your fifties, not in your forties. I had a swollen prostate. A lot of men my age don't like to talk about it, because of insecurities, and they're ashamed to let somebody know that they were experiencing sexual erection problems. Come to find out, it was a prostate problem with me.

"I think my generation had a big problem going to the doctors because of hearing all those men talk about the Tuskegee syphilis experiments. There is no doubt about it. I would like to be sexually active in my sixties and seventies. So I'm trying to change some habits. I quit smoking, but I still eat too much red meat. I see what's happening to my friends. We used to play pickup (basketball) games. Now most of us can't do that. Some have come down with sickness. Another friend has liver problems because of drinking too much. Another was a smoker and now has lung problems. Another has high blood pressure and high cholesterol and has to watch his diet. I never had to think about those things before."

In addition to physical health issues, there are also financial health issues. Despite having more income and wealth than generations before them, older black men recognize that their financial situation allows them only so much freedom. All this plays out in Morgan's life, despite his insistence that he and other men are not facing a midlife crisis. After his divorce, Morgan was thrown back into the pool of single black men, but he was not the same person. He was not the same person physically and didn't feel as attractive to women.

He is no longer slim and good-looking in his opinion, as he was when he was younger, before he got married. His waistline has grown, he is losing his hair, and as result Morgan sees himself as not as desirable to women—younger women in particular. He also is not the same person financially. He is making close to six figures in salary, but nearing age fifty, he sees his career as having peaked. So he has two contradictory things working in his life at the same time: the physical aging process that makes him less attractive to women, but also his financial aging, which allows him to have more options—at least for now.

Brazil allows him to go back and go forth between these contradictions in a seamless way because his financial situation gives him access to women who would not normally find him attractive in the States.

Sexual Healing: The Bridge between Men's Physical and Mental Health

Some of the most recent research on men's health shows that the male penis is sort of a thermometer, or "dipstick," of a man's overall health. The quality or lack of quality of a man's erection can be a strong indicator of his cardiovascular, metabolic, and mental health.

As they age, men explore things with their minds to prop up their bodies. Some of this has to do with the fact that their body does not act the way it used to. So, despite that men's sexual response system is often thought of as just biological, older men tend to resort to fantasies more to get them sexually aroused.

Contrary to what Morgan thinks, fantasies don't have to be the "forbidden fruit" of a man's heart, or a "Pandora's box" of secrets that men keep close to the heart. In fact, there is nothing wrong with sexual fantasies at all. Most professionals agree that the *absence* of sexual fantasies is a problem. Sexual fantasies are simply erotic images or mental representations that get played out.

Research on sexual fantasies demonstrates that men regularly have at least forty sexual fantasies such as sleeping with a woman other than his partner, women dressed in erotic clothing, being tied up and sexually stimulated by a woman, or having a penis so large that it penetrates a large vagina.

Sexual fantasies can be as simple as role playing with one's partner: playing doctor, using sex toys, or just having sex in different places throughout the house or outside the house. Sexual fantasies simply stimulate sexual arousal. So for men, the problem with sexual fantasies tends to be *not* having them. And while all men engage in sexual fantasies, older men approach their sexual fantasies in ways that allow them more access to them. Here is how Morgan described his last trip to Brazil:

> *She was posing and having a good time. She went and got vegetables out of the kitchen and brought that into the bedroom. I always eat my vegetables. And she had them in places I never imagined vegetables going. It was a ball!*
>
> *She was the first woman I ever been with who had plastic surgery; she had breast implants. So that was different; that was way different for me. The next day, about noon, the girl that I had met on Sunday called me and asked me if I wanted her to come over. Of course I told her to come over. So we're sitting on the couch, watching TV, and just talking, and she said, "Do you remember my friend ____?" I said, "Yeah, I remember her."*

"Do you mind if she comes over?"

So I get this silly grin.

"You got to pay her cab fare," she told me.

"How much is it?" I asked.

She told me it was five bucks.

"Bring her ass over!" I said.

Man, those two girls turned me out. I don't know what the hell. The one girl by herself was something, but the two of them, they wore me out—almost put my ass in a coma. Then they got up. They cleaned my apartment. They asked for some money to go to the grocery store; they went and bought food and then cooked it. Now, you know, I kind of felt bad; I couldn't really handle them like I thought I should. Once they got to sucking my dick and sucking my nipples, I was coming all over the place. I hit it again and this time I hit them both—while I'm sucking and licking on one, I was thrusting on the other.

This had always been one of my fantasies, and I didn't even have to suggest it to live it out.

Saturday night, the two girls came back. I was ready for them that time. I took a Viagra and I put them both to sleep. I was impressed myself when I hit her in the ass, it was good. It was real good. I mean, I thought about her and the girl I called for weeks. I'm in bed most nights trying to get some sleep, and that memory flashes and my dick gets hard.

"Damn, man, go to sleep!"

Morgan's sexual fantasies were met in a variety of ways: a threesome, anal sex, women who like to do things with vegetables, women with breast implants. Morgan had so many of his sexual options met that he felt as if God had granted him his last wish—a sort of "last meal" request before taking him to glory.

This is important because living out these fantasies gives men the belief that they are actually really *living* before they die. It's not just about getting hard and being aroused; it's about life itself. For men, the idea of living before dying and not leaving anything undone is real. Morgan, however, was far from the only man to report on his sexual fantasies. For some, the fantasy had to do with the looks of the women.

> *I was having sex with what I would call a fantasy fuck, and the reason I say that is because the woman looked famous. This chick looked like Nicole Ari Parker from* Soul Food *(the one who plays the attorney). It was everything I imagined. I hit her so hard, the condom broke.*

A "fantasy fuck" for this gentleman was important because it allowed him to get closer to images that he sees regularly on TV but that were inaccessible to him before. For another man, it was the opportunity to have sex with women seen in porno videos. This was a different type of star, but again, an example of the type of coveted experience that men seek to have with women who are *televisual* in their appeal. What Brazil does is take away the secrecy of sexual fantasies and allow for them to be explored more openly. As one man said, "You could live like Caligula. I'm talking about dancing girls and bringing on the midgets, and everything!" In contrast, in the States, men go to great lengths to explore their sexuality with phone sex, Internet sex, and video sex.

Brazilian Context: The Epiphany of Lust

Most men, whether older or younger, agree that everything is on the table sexually in Brazil. All types of fetishes, addictions, and obsessions can be acted out. Brazil allows for those fantasies to become reality. The erotic imagery, ideas, or stories that men have been playing out in their minds can all be played out in real life in Brazil. And with the advent of drugs like Viagra, Levitra, and Cialis, older men can act these experiences out for as long as they want or, as Morgan says, "for as long as they want to hear those young girls moan."

Another important issue is that Brazil essentially creates sexual fantasies for men to explore, so that in addition to having a lot of sex, men are all but compelled to explore more sexual options. This is often discussed as a part of the transition. As one top executive said, "On the first day you are more or less caught with your mouth wide open because you can't believe it."

So a guy might start off having sex with multiple women on his first night, and by the second night he might try something more exotic. As Gerald, a senior vice president of sales from Atlanta, said, "On my first night I hit three; on my second night I had two sisters." Consequently, doing things sexually they had never done before becomes a large part of the experience. This is important because sexual fantasies don't just come out of nowhere. What Brazil does is set in motion the idea of sexual options even if men were not aware of them. So whereas Morgan was aware of what was in his heart, most men are encouraged to explore their sexual options simply because of the amount of sex that is available to them.

You can think of the sexual fantasies as going through various stages in Brazil. First, for most men, the sexual fantasy simply involves having lots of sex with women who would normally be beyond their reach.

"There is no such thing as 'I don't do that' (in Brazil)," said Gerald. "The next time I go, I might try three women at a time!"

Culture of Younger Women

Despite all the variety and exposure to sexual experiences that older men find in Brazil, there was one constant: younger women. While most men enjoyed sex with women ten, twenty, and even thirty years younger than they, none had sex with underage women, but they all had sex with women younger than they were. So the exposure to sexual variety normally did not extend to age variety. It might have been variety in looks, number, or positions, but not variety in age.

What this brings up again is that older men have been affected by the idea that being with younger women sexually is the ultimate testament to their youth but also the best indication of their sexual appetites. The disinterest in older women sexually and the almost paranoid interest in young women, as exemplified in Morgan's case, is probably the most consistent motivating factor in older adult men's sexuality. In addition to penis size, age is the ultimate cock blocker.

For Morgan, one of the primary ways this played out was in his assessment of the role of money in his and other men's ability to attract women. Without the aid of natural good looks, and the realization of a peaking career, Morgan was almost delusional in his belief that money would make him attractive to younger women. On one hand, the reality of older men and younger women is such a staple in modern society that it seems to go without saying. If a guy is older, and lucky enough or able enough, he can snag a younger woman.

Thomas, a college administrator who is fifty-five years old and dating a twenty-two-year-old woman, explains it this way:

> *Guys want females younger than them for a couple of reasons—not just because of the physical, but because of the mental and emotional, as well. Guys look for younger women because they want balance and they want to be in a position of control. Older women kind of get set in their ways. Once they get to a certain age, their tolerance for different things shorten and change. Younger women don't know any difference. I can introduce her to things she's never been introduced to before. That's exciting for both of us.*
>
> *Women my age have baggage, just like I got baggage. The younger women treats me kind. Before I even get off from work, she's calling me, asking me what I want for dinner. When I get home, my bath is ready. When I get out of the bath, she's there to give me a foot rub. Then she's ready to get in any*

position I want, [sexually] as long as I want. Call it what you want, but anyone who has a problem with it is jealous.

Conclusion

When does a black man hit middle age? If you go simply by national mortality rates for black men—which is age sixty-five—then middle age is around thirty-three. And while this may just be a technical point, it raises more general questions.

When do black men start to deal with the realities of growing older? How do black men deal with issues of decline in their attractiveness to women? How do they deal with the reality of their limited financial capabilities and sense of failure in their jobs or careers? And, perhaps most important, how do black men, who have stood at the pinnacle of the physicality mountain compared with other men, (tall, dark, handsome, and packing) and who have often put a lot of their personal identity into their sexual prowess, deal with the decline in their sexual functioning?

These are not questions that black men often deal with, nor do most people consider these questions when they think about black men. Most of the focus is on the trauma of black men dying at an early age due to homicide, suicide, or AIDS (the leading cause of death). However, for Thomas and Morgan and the majority of black men who live past "middle age," life becomes a very different experience.

The French phrase for orgasm is *la petite mort*, which literally means "little death." For older men, sex is a tenuous connection to life. Sex becomes one of the main corridors that older black professional men use to look into their lives and evaluate what they have done and what they want to do before they die. For older black men, sexual fantasies become one of the major things they rely on to connect them to the past and their future. The problem with fantasies is that often these sexual acts and ideas conflict with the sexual acts and ideas that they think older black women are willing to participate in.

Another problem with older black men trying to live the lifestyle of younger men is that this does not give younger black men any elders to look up to. In addition, it robs older black women of viable options as soul mates and spouses. When men like Morgan go to Brazil to live out sexual fantasies with younger women, or men like Morgan choose to date women who are twenty-plus years their junior, they are ruining the balance within their community—they are stripping away the very foundation.

It's okay to grow old, and it's more than okay to explore your sexuality as an older man. But there are many ways to do that—it doesn't have to be at the expense of contemporary black women.

The current narrow conception of male sexuality with aging does not encourage adult men to accept and enact *adult* masculinity—they are emulating and trying to be "young." Although "senior sex" might sound funny, it should not be considered nasty, dirty, or an insult. Only through engaging will men stop blaming older black women and start looking at the changing reality of their own lives.

Chapter Five

She Acts Like a Man

I think one of the things a lot of white women—and a lot of women outside of the United States, for that matter—do well is that they know how to play their role. It's not that they're totally passive. But these women fight their battles a different way. They catch more flies with honey and they're not going head-to-head. Yeah, I know it's a trick. But I don't care if I'm fooled. I'm fat and [happy].

I think the thing is with a lot of sisters, is that they want to let you know what the boundaries are and what they're not going to do. I think the good brothers here, realistically (and this is going to sound like I'm putting all the blame on women), are just tired of fighting them. I know I'm tired of the scowl when I just try to say hello. I'm tired of them being out in groups and being immediately judged by them. It takes a lot for a man to walk over to a group of women and approach them.

I have seen a lot of angry women. And they're angry for whatever reason. I understand that you may not know me personally. Maybe I might look like somebody who did her wrong in the past. I think a lot of us just come to the point where we're not going to fight through all that.

It's so much work with [black women]. I'm tired of negotiating, too. That's the thing that blew me away when I got to Brazil. The girls there—there was no work. It's that angry-black-woman syndrome that is preventing many a good relationship from getting off the ground.

I know a couple of women, beautiful women, who will always be alone because they're angry and you can feel the force field from ten feet away . . . you can feel it. And sometimes, I don't think they have a clue that this is what they are doing to brothers. I have to say that to stay positive about them, because if I believed that if they knew what they were doing and still did it, I'd lose faith in all of them. So I have to believe that they just don't know what they're doing. That's why I'm telling them.

We don't have to negotiate everything in a relationship. Women who've always been a head of something, there's negotiation all the time. There are some things I'm not going to negotiate with.

One time, I was getting out of the shower and I started putting on lotion. The girl grabbed the lotion bottle, and it wasn't for [show]. She started lotioning my feet—something small. I think men, a lot of us, are nurturing people. We like to nurture but we also want it reciprocated, you know. If the softer, gentler sex is harsh, where do we go from there?

It's great that (black women) are survivors. But they don't have to tell you up front, "I don't need you!"—that I'm replaceable. When I'm in Brazil, I'm not trying to fight and compete to be dominant. They let me nurture them and take

*care of them. I don't hear "I got it!" or "I can get it myself!" or
"I can do it!" They let you treat them like ladies.*

*If a woman wants to be nurtured, shut your mouth and
let it happen. But, you know, at the same time, you've got to
be willing to reciprocate. You can't be this modern woman and
then when it's not convenient for you, all of a sudden you're
Betty Crocker. You know, let us know what we're getting, and
be consistent about it.*

—Keith, 42, business owner, Atlanta

Keith has been to Brazil six times in the last five
years. He says that he tries to go at least once
a year.

"I do a lot of consulting and contractual work, so I have a
pretty flexible schedule and I go between contracts as often as
I can," he said.

He first heard about Brazil in 1997, from a group of his
business acquaintances at one of the many popular black networking events in Atlanta. Like a lot of men, it took him a
while before he actually took his first trip in 2000. He was
recently divorced at the time and was already tired of the dating scene, so when one of his buddies brought up the idea, he
was ready.

Considering where Keith lives, Atlanta, dubbed the "Black
Mecca," it is not as if he didn't have a lot of exposure and ac-

cess to black women. One 2004 study of Atlanta found that in the city, there were 579 black males for every thousand black women. There are 346 unmarried, employed black men for every 1,000 black women, and 710 black men with graduate or professional degrees for every 1,000 black women with graduate or professional degrees.

Keith was one of the first men who helped me understand the one dynamic that made absolutely no sense when I first began to listen to men talk about their experiences with Brazilian women. His experiences also helped put in perspective the recent studies that suggested why married black women report such poor quality in their marriages and why some actually have worse outcomes when compared to single black women. One study, "The Consequences of Marriage for African Americans," noted, "In fact, married black women are significantly less likely to report having excellent health than are unmarried black women. These findings are unexpected and beg for explanation. One credible explanation is that the marriages of African Americans often subject them to conflict and stress."

The paradox that originally made no sense was that most of the women with whom these black men said they were having deep and personal interactions and relationships often didn't speak English. At first, I didn't get it. How can you have a deep relationship with someone you can't communicate with? I thought it was the greatest contradiction and that it undermined all they were saying about how profound and meaningful their experiences were. But the more I listened, the more it started to make sense. The inability or limited ability of Brazilian women to communicate verbally with black American men was precisely what the trip represented for many men—a break from black women's voices.

For Keith, being underrepresented in Atlanta also meant that he was overexposed to the voices and issues of black women, and it was if, by not hearing a black woman's voice, he didn't have to hear all the history and blame and shame that has been involved in black male-female relationships.

Brazilian women didn't speak English and therefore could not have conversations with black men. And it was not perceived as a language *problem*. Just the opposite. What Brazilian women and African-American men didn't communicate verbally was powerfully and perfectly communicated through mannerisms and interactions—which, for a lot of black men, said much more than words ever could. Through nonverbal communication, black men heard at least three things loud and clear: (1) black women could be strong and sexual but at the expense of their femininity and sensuality; (2) black women's attitude and anger are the core of their identity and something they relish; and (3) black women are in constant competition, and their lack of submission is the major source of conflict in relationships.

Based on what men talked about consistently, it was clear that they enjoyed being with Brazilian women—not only sexually but also emotionally.

"I just liked being with them, looking at them . . . and being in their presence," said Michael, from Houston.

That is why black men would do things like kiss, hold hands, take walks on the beach, perform oral sex, and do other things—things black women constantly complain about their men *not* doing—with these women in Brazil. The reason black men were able to do this was because they felt elevated in all their senses—touch, taste, and smell—as men.

This is what Keith was referring to when he said men are more nurturing. They felt able to open up to their own senses and affections in ways they could not back in America. The irony, of course, is that not only did they receive affection, but they also gave affection, perhaps more than they did in their relationships with black women.

However, no matter how many times men talked about how different Brazilian women are and how much they "know how to treat a man" and "let a man be a man," I really didn't understood how these women are so different from black women in America until a brother, who worked in law enforcement, went into a monologue about how femininity is dead among black women. He had come to this conclusion based on his travels to Brazil and parts of Southeast Asia.

At one point in the conversation he sort of broke down and blurted out, "[Sisters] be shaving their head and wearing tattoos! Half the time it feels like you're messing with another *man*."

What he was getting at was the duality of sexism against black women, in that they have been made into sexual objects but have been masculinized at the same time.

Historically, black women have always been thought of as sexual objects. That's why a Lorraine Hansburg could write, "I can be coming home from eight hours on an assembly line or fourteen hours in Mrs. Halsey's kitchen. I can be filled up that day with three hundred years of rage so that my eyes are flashing and my flesh is trembling—and with boys in the streets, they look at me and think of sex. They look at me and that's all they think."

The reality is that black women's sexuality was rarely based on their femininity. This is what Sojourner Truth addressed in her famous speech "Ain't I a Woman?" Black women have been denied the pristine stature of femininity that was accorded to white women.

In contrast, Latin American women have always been conceptualized as both sexual and sensual. The key difference is their femininity, a femininity that was deeply influenced by the idea that they submitted to the will of men—a point emphasized below by an online service promoting Latin American women (www.latin-wife.com):

International Introductions: The American Man's Alternative to American Women:

It is common knowledge that Latin American women are faithful, loyal, and devoted wives. There is a reason why Colombia has the lowest divorce rate in the world; their world is centered on the family. Colombian women stay with their first family until marriage and then the tradition continues with their new family. They have been raised to complement, nurture and respect their men. My own experience attests to this. Colombian women, even the ones in impoverished conditions, are positive, open minded, happy, playful, fun, spontaneous, warm and affectionate . . .

What this advertisement pointed to was that the allure of Latin American women is that they appeal to men's senses—their own sensuality. And femininity, which is not the same thing as docility, is the thing that does it. South American women are also characterized as sassy and passionate, especially sexually. So the issue is not attitude alone. Women can be granted attitude as long as it doesn't cross the border into masculinity. For example, in the hierarchy of offensive remarks toward women, being called a bitch is an insult, but it is still a feminine insult. That's why it's offensive for a man to call another man a bitch; because it's equated with femininity.

However, when a man calls a woman a dyke or a lesbian, he is challenging her essence as a woman. Attitude is actually a valued trait among Brazilian women that African-American men interact with. That's why the "girlfriend experience" is a widely acknowledged phenomenon. In the girlfriend experience, if a woman sees a man she has not seen for a while or even if they recently met, she acts jealous and possessive of him. Her jealousy and attitude do not offend the man but actually are endearing. It confirms that he's the object of her desire. Despite how aggressive and brazen Brazilian women are known to be, they are still considered sensual. As Keith mentioned, these women were not passive; they just fight their battles in different ways. According to him, they catch more "flies with honey" and don't go "head-to-head." Who goes head-to-head? Sisters!

She Has an Attitude!

Brazilian women make much better wives than American women. An American woman has several fundamental problems that will never go away and that will get much worse a few years after she is married:

Her inherent anti-male bias and pre-occupation with fairness that was drilled into her in high school, college, and through the media. Her constant confrontations and trying to prove herself and to make a point. Her self-centeredness, her ridiculously high expectations, her sense of entitlement, her high-maintenance, superficial, and stuck up attitude, her snootiness and her sense of superiority. This "princess" syndrome means that she will always think that she is better than you, and that she deserves and she is entitled to whatever she wants from you. Her using sex as a weapon and reward to get things. Brazilian women generally don't have any of these problems. Marrying an American woman simply does not make sense.

The ONLY reason men stay with American women is because they did not have enough exposure to Brazilian women. Any man who spent a few months in Brazil will not even look at American women again.

—NoMarriage.com

According to Ronald, a physician practicing in Baltimore, black women are the only women in the world known for their attitude.

"Where else in the world is a black woman's attitude accepted as the social norm, except in America?" he asked. "I've met German women, I've met South American women, I've met Central American women, and I've met Asian women. No where else can you snap your finger, roll your eyes, and get loud in public and that's considered socially acceptable and something you're allowed to do and no one will check you for it, except in America. I find it as a negative. And I do get that American women are the pinnacle of the social forefront of social gains, political gains, interpersonal gains, but the reality is, when it gets right down to basics of human relationships, you feel you have the right to socially embarrass your man, get loud, act as ugly as you want in public. I find that as a turn off."

What Ronald talks about, I've heard many times. Black women have become the world's anti-example of feminine traits. Unlike Asian women, who are "orientalized" as being "humble, flowers, delicate, or diminutive," or Latin American women, who are "Latinized" as "happy and playful," black women are "African-Americanized" as loud, talkative, competitive, hard, and harsh to the point of being masculine. Like Keith, Ronald experienced black women's core identity as based on attitude. And what he found particularly unattractive was how black women act in public.

"I feel, as my own personal experiences, that black women feel like they've earned the right to act ugly in public," Ronald said. "I don't agree with that. I'm tired of black American women. Maybe it's because of the black American woman who has become so strong and so dominant and so fortified in their opinions and who they are that they won't let a man be a man.

"I've had women that won't let me open doors for them. I know you can open your own door; your arms aren't broken. But can you just let me be chivalrous? Let me be a gentleman! That's not appreciated. I was raised to say 'please' and 'thank you.' And I've had women tell me, 'You say please too much! That attitude gets on my nerves.' I don't enjoy attitude. I don't want to fight all the time. Look, I'm not too stressed. I like what I do. I'm financially well off. I love to travel. I have good friends. I don't keep drama in my life. So when a woman comes to me with drama, particularly black women, I'm not attracted to that."

In contrast to being complementary and supportive of men's role, black women are independent of those roles. The issue of black women's independence points to one of the fundamental dynamics about the experience of African-American men in Brazil. It confirms to them not only what black women don't do but also what black men are not allowed to do. When Keith was saying that he wished black women would "just shut up," he was invoking this idea that men *naturally* want to provide. Similarly, when Ronald was arguing to "let me be a gentleman," it pointed out that not only do some men want to be served, but they also want to serve. So what makes the Brazil experience so potent is that it allowed black men to see both sides of what they felt was wrong with black women's attitudes.

On one hand, men like Keith want to see themselves as "traditional" and as providers, but there are also men like Ronald, who want to see themselves as "gentlemen" and as catering to the needs of women. Consequently, the reason why black women's attitude is experienced as widely offensive is because it doesn't allow a spectrum of men, from those who are "traditional" to those who claim to be "gentlemen," to assume their roles.

When a black woman asserts her independence, in the eyes of black men not only is she rejecting those who want to control or provide for her, but she is also rejecting those men who would like to cater to her as well. This is ultimately what Keith found offensive when faced with the claim "I'm replaceable," and what Ronald found unattractive. Men spend their entire lives not just wanting to be treated a certain way, but they also want to perform in a certain way. This is something that black men, from powder puffs to gangstas and thugs, see black women's impendence denying them.

In addition to black women's attitude, there is black women's anger. In complete contrast to the warm and affectionate demeanor of Latin American women, the most prominent characteristic of black women is anger. To prove this point, one man actually sent me a link to the Web site the angryblack woman.com. The archetype of this image of the angry black woman is Condoleezza Rice, who is made fun of for a variety of reasons in African-American life. But as a symbol, she represents all that is wrong with black women: angry, alone, with bad hair, childless, and in alliance with whites.

What is significant to note is that both Keith and Ronald seemed to acknowledge black women's anger in a positive way. They seemed to acknowledge that black women's anger comes from a unique history in America and in relationships with black men. The issue, as they perceived it, was black women's inability or unwillingness to see black men as individuals. Rather, there was a feeling of collective blame of all black men, which led to an inordinate amount of work, which neither was willing to put up with.

The problem with this is that men like Keith and Ronald tend to emphasize black women's anger as judging and making them immediately guilty to black women. Clearly, this is a part of their experience and plays some role in how they choose to interact. However, focusing on that alone or mainly actually minimizes the struggles of black women, and it robs black men of the potential to have empathy for black women's reality. So while both Keith and Ronald appear to acknowledge black women's anger, they are also dismissive of it. What this does is continue a very narrow and simplistic understanding of the uniqueness of black women's attitudes while denying their pain and anger at the same time.

I should mention that in conversations with black men, there are a lot of ideas about the thing we refer to as "black women's attitudes." Some of the more prominent theories about why black women have attitudes are (a) black women are used to running things, and when they come in contact with a strong man they don't know how to act; (b) black women have been hurt so many times that they don't know how to give individual men a chance, because all black men are seen as guilty until proven innocent; (c) black women are not raised by fathers and, as a result, don't know how to treat a man; (d) black women have been influenced by feminist ideologies that don't allow men to be men. There are even theories of their sexuality.

Of all the theories, the idea that black women are influenced by feminist ideologies is one of the most powerful, because it suggests that black women have an awareness and a certain indulgence for their behaviors. It's what Ronald found so offensive, and it was the thing that gave Keith some hope so that he would not lose faith in them. The idea that black women have adopted ideas about what a "strong black woman" is, how that influences the way she acts, is perplexing to some men.

As one publications director pointed out:

You have all these articles and television shows about how brothers can't handle the strong black woman. And what is the real definition of a strong black woman? A woman who can argue real well? And who wants that in a relationship, anyway? I'm thinking a strong, black woman is a woman that understands. Yes, she has the authority and she's got her job and she may be equal or more intelligent than her mate. But for the sake of her marriage, she understands that sometimes she has to acquiesce because the traditional roles of men being a man—being head of a household, as well as holding a job, having to deal with being a professional black man, having to deal with racism, discrimination, people not taking you as seriously unless you've got certain super credentials—shouldn't have to come with coming home and dealing with the same stress. It just doesn't make sense. In my opinion, a strong black woman understands what it takes to make her mate happy and, in turn, hopefully, a strong black man understands the same thing.

Others argue that the media is mostly to blame for black women's ideas about being strong. Greg in L.A., whom we will hear more from, said:

I equate all of this to the beginning of Oprah Winfrey. I'm serious, man. Malcolm X used to talk about the power of a person speaking in public and people listening. When you have the public's eye—and in this case, Oprah had our women's eyes or ears; she filled them in the beginning with how a man ain't shit, how a man will cheat on you, how a man will fuck your best friend—you have a lot of power to control how that person thinks. It got to the point where men are just seen as untrustworthy. You can't trust a man; Oprah told them that.

In my personal life, I was with a woman at that time that watched Oprah at four o'clock every day and tested it on me when I got home. Every episode, she came at me with the stuff [she had seen on Oprah]. I found myself being a recipient of that nonsense on a daily basis.

Not surprisingly, this same woman went on to say that the reason why black men love Brazil so much is because there's no Oprah and no Winfrey in Brazil. That's true. There ain't no

*woman down there trying to give you a woman's view on life
and all the rest of that blah, blah, blah!*

How black men think of the cause or source of black
women's attitudes partly determines how they will respond
to them. Men typically don't reference the wide spectrum of
black women's attitudes, which are unique in America and
in the world. Research consistently shows, for example, that
black women are unique in their attitudes toward freedom,
justice, and gender equity. Specifically, black women are
found to have some of the highest support levels for affirmative action, group-based remedies for oppression, and rejection of individual explanations for the origins of inequality.
More important, black women are often found to have high
levels of support for the plight of black men, according to
a recent poll by Harvard, the *Washington Post,* and Kaiser.
Presumably, these attitudes would make black women more
"attractive," to use Ronald's language. What this brings up
is that the biggest unearthed area is not black women's attitudes, but black *men's* attitudes.

Black Men's Attitudes

When applied to black women, the term "attitude" typically
refers to the way that black women as a group carry themselves in an outward fashion—particularly in public settings,
as Ronald was quick to point out. However, the term simply refers to how an individual comes to make a favorable or
unfavorable evaluation of a situation. This is an important

distinction because one of the tricks that have been played on black women is that they have been labeled with having an "attitude," while the attitudes of black men have gone un-examined.

In fact, it is likely the attitudes of black men that deter-mine their unfavorable experience with black women's atti-tudes.

Black men, and middle-class and professional black men in particular, have some of the most restrictive ideas about black women's role in the family and in society compared to other groups. Studies show that black men, both professional and nonprofessional, have liberal attitudes toward race when compared to other groups. However, black men—specifically middle-class and professional black men—have been found to have less liberal attitudes toward women's roles when com-pared with whites. In fact, not only have middle-class and professional black men been found to have more restrictive ideas about women's roles when compared with white men, but also compared with nonprofessional black men. Studies actually show that poor and working poor black men, those who presumably have ghetto masculinity, actually have less restrictive attitudes about black women's roles than do their brethren who have middle-class and professional jobs.

What this suggests is that middle-class and professional black men face a "provider" role strain, not because they lack the financial resources that would allow them to assume their roles. Rather, it is because they have financial resources that they expect to assume traditional roles. Many middle-class and professional black men feel that they have earned the right to make decisions and that black women should follow suit. Todd in Boston stated:

"If you're a professional black man—you're running all these companies and making these decisions—how are you going to come home and do what your wife says? I'm not saying don't do what your wife says, but how's your wife going to have the final decision in that relationship?"

A businessman who has been going to Brazil for more than a decade was even more explicit on this point:

"Black women always want to talk about commitment, but they don't want to talk about obedience," he said. "You will never hear a woman in Brazil talk about how they don't want or don't need a man."

This attitude about submission and obedience reflects a type of "black machismo" that rarely gets acknowledged. Another man expressed his confusion about why black women won't submit in this way.

"God holds me accountable for everything that goes on in my house," said Phillip, a graphic designer. "So I make the final decisions. That doesn't mean I don't listen to what you say. When I told the woman that I was dating about this, she couldn't handle that. And I asked her, what if I make great decisions? Well, that didn't make a difference. She said she would be a fool to do that. And I said, 'Well, wait a minute. Why?' I said. 'You don't have a problem submitting to your boss at work. You don't have a problem submitting to your pastor; why would you have a problem submitting to me?' "

A medical technician in Charlotte, North Carolina, echoed a similar sentiment:

"Right now, I work in lab; I battle over minuscule things every day like you wouldn't believe," he said. "When I come home, I don't want to fight with my woman. I want peace in my home, and I want a woman that would suit me, don't you?"

The tendency to confuse lack of submission with lack of support, and lack of peace with competition, is what explains the intense conflict in relationships.

Competition, Conflict, and Castration

African-Americans not only have the lowest marriage rate of any racial group in the United States; they also have the lowest quality of marriages. Studies show that African-Americans are less likely to be happy in marriages and that black women are less likely to be fulfilled in their relationships. In fact, one study on the quality of black versus white marriages reported, "Blacks are significantly more likely to report that the spouse has affairs, hits or pushes, wastes money, or does not make them feel love."

More than twenty years of research on marital outcomes demonstrates that it is not the "number of differences" between partners, or the "frequency of arguing" that leads to marital breakups. Rather, it is how couples *handle* the arguments. As one researcher asserted, "It is the immediacy of the interchange between two people that most directly affects the story of marriage over time."

A lot of this is due to conflict and stress caused by men like Keith, who feels that he is in competition with black women.

The question becomes, competition over what? Clearly a lot of things can be the source of stress, but the issue is competition over dominion. Who actually has ultimate control, and what does one have to go through to get it?

Going back to the reality and consequences of not focusing on black men's attitudes, perhaps the biggest trick has been not focusing on black men's anger, when in fact, black men's anger, like black men's rage, is the source of much of what they experience. One of the most dubious things that has happened is that although women experience a whole range of emotions, black women have been reduced to being characterized as experiencing only anger. Men, on the other hand, often experience only a small set of emotions, and black men are not talking about their anger at all. Why? Because to acknowledge anger is often to talk about something that you are unable to control.

Anger and rage are often just a form of social impotence that men feel about situations and circumstances that they cannot control.

The same *Washington Post* survey showed that when asked how often in the past month they have felt "unable to control the important things in your life," black men had higher percentages in the "very often" and "somewhat often" categories— higher than black women, white men, and white women. When asked about a list of things people worry about, black men scored consistently higher on the "very worried" category than any other group. This makes black men sensitive to the struggles they have, and one of the primary reasons why they experience so much conflict in their relationships with black women.

The reality is that black men have attitudes about a whole range of topics that have not been explored, and because they have not, they have been allowed to focus on the attitudes of others—especially black women. And these attitudes are often the source of conflict in relationships with black women that men are increasingly choosing not to deal with.

Conclusion

Recent research suggests that men are attracted to subordinate women. The research findings suggest that accomplished women may be at a further disadvantage because powerful men prefer to marry "less accomplished women." This was the basis for Maureen Dowd's controversial book *Are Men Necessary?* But rarely did this book get mentioned in black America. Given the recent controversy over the Don Imus debacle (where he lost his job for referring to members of the Rutgers women's basketball team as "nappy-headed ho's"), it is rather interesting that at the same time that these young ladies of Rutgers would be lauded as such great examples, they are the very kind of accomplished black women that black men avoid the most. Poor black women may be "ho's," but accomplished, educated, and articulate black women are competitive, unattractive, and masculine. They are the ones whom many men avoid.

In many ways, black men's experiences with Brazilian women are the exact opposite of their experiences with African-American women. When black men hear Brazilian women's voices, they hear love and affirmation. When they hear black women's voices, they hear judgment and shame. When black men see themselves in Brazilian women's eyes, they see desire. When black men see themselves in black women's eyes, they see judgment and blame. When they look at Brazilian women, they see strong women who are also feminine. They might be prostitutes, but at least they are women.

There are several issues at play when it comes to how men respond to black women's anger and attitude. First is the issue of whether they understand it. The second is whether, even if they do understand, they choose to deal with it. The third is whether black men ever acknowledge their own attitude and anger as the basis for their interactions with black women.

In the first issue, reminiscent of the movie *The Upside of Anger*, which depicted the issues that some men face with loving a "difficult" woman, the question for black men is whether they can see the pain that some black women may use as a defense mechanism to protect themselves from further harm. Given the disproportionate rates of physical and sexual violence that black women face, it's not only heartbreak that some black women are trying to protect themselves against.

For men, this doesn't mean looking past what they experience as attitude, but recognizing that behind the anger is pain and trauma, and that perhaps there is something there to build on.

In the second issue, if men do have this understanding, can they then acknowledge the privilege that allows them possibly not to care and to choose to exempt themselves from the opportunity to be in relationships? As opposed to talking about what they are not willing to do, can they acknowledge that black women's pain is an extension of their oppression, which is then compounded by their decisions not to be in partnership with them? The issue is whether someone like Keith could ever express his hurt at being judged and whether he can take ownership of what he thinks black women don't know about him.

Can black men look into their *own* attitudes, which make them want to perform in certain social and sexual ways? Research has shown that black men's attitudes can lead to a number of psychometric variables such as "restrictive emotionality," "restrictive affectionate behavior between men," and "conflicts between work and family relations." Black men, especially middle-class and professional black men, have been infected with ideas of power, success, and competition. Do we see that their own attitudes and anger are the basis for conflict, competition, castration, and a whole constellation of other feelings that they have? Said more plainly, can they plug into their own attitudes and not use them to blame black women or other black men who choose not to follow those attitudes?

Finally, African-American men don't see the love in the independence that black women have been identified with. They see the assertion of independence as a rejection of themselves, and they are threatened and hurt by that. One of the interesting dynamics about blaming and shaming is that this attitude is always on the prowl for additional targets to help fortify its own position. So if it is not black women who are to blame, it is other black men who don't follow suit—specifically, other brothers who choose to stay in relationships with black women.

One of the things men consistently talked about was not just the attitudes of black women but also the attitudes of black men who did not respond the way they themselves chose to.

Chapter Six

The Frigid Black Woman

To be honest, I find that black women are very inhibited sexually. In my last relationship, there was no oral sex. She loved to have it performed on her, though. But she found it disgusting to do it. They don't mind you taking care of them, but when you go to put the microphone in their face, all of a sudden they can't sing.

It's just their perspective on sex. I talk to women, and I ask them what they will do and what they won't do sexually. The one thing I look for is when a woman says, "Yeah, I'll do that if my man wants it." That's unattractive. She's not doing it because she likes it or because she enjoys it; she's only doing it because that's what she thinks her man wants. There is a difference.

I had a couple of sexual interludes with a friend of mine. We weren't going together or anything, but the sex was incredible. On the very first night she just brought a hundred percent. I didn't have to tell her that I wanted oral sex. It was like an urge. You want to feel that way in bed. You want to feel *uninhibited. But if she is coming half-ass and not enjoying it and into it, it's not good for me.*

Oral sex is a big thing for men. Our equipment is special to us, but if you are going to treat it like a used car, if this is something you don't enjoy, then don't do it. You have black women who treat it like it's work. They're like, "Let me hurry up and do this so he can go to sleep and leave me alone!" I avoid those women.

In Brazil, this is not a problem. The majority of the women enjoy what they're doing. It is very fulfilling for a man who finds himself in bed with an attractive, long-hair, nonfake type of woman, who is really responding sexually, as opposed to a black woman who is asking, "What can you bring me," and "What are you going to do for me?"

You can feel the detachment in what some women do in bed, like there is a bit of humiliation in what they do, and they show that. One woman told me flat out that she never had to pay for dinner, that her boyfriends always took care of that. She was so proud of that. At the same time, she was a dud in bed. It drove me to the point where I was questioning why the hell were they paying for her dinner. She wasn't bringing shit.

I've been with a lot of women. And going to places like Brazil and the Dominican Republic has made that number substantial [laughter]. Speaking from a male perspective, it's about accessibility to very attractive women who aim to please, who allow you to explore your sexuality without criticism or denial, without being snubbed or inhibited.

—Derrick, 42, engineer, Houston

Black women, like black men, have always been set apart for their sexuality. Viewed as either Jezebels or Sapphires, black women have long been considered in Western culture in relationship to their "explosive" sexuality, their looseness, their lustfulness, and their insatiable sexual appetite, like the female lead in Spike Lee's *She's Gotta Have It*.

As a result of this view of black women, in popular culture a sort of sexual hierarchy of "once you go black, you'll never go back" has historically applied to them and to black men, too. However, the exalting of black female sexuality is all ancient history for men like Derrick, who travel to Brazil. Derrick, an engineer, makes a good living and disagrees vehemently with the notion that black women are the pinnacle of sexuality. According to him and others, black women today are not very sexual at all. In fact, they have a number of sexual inhibitions that don't allow them to explore their sexuality fully. More than anything, it is their attitudes toward sex that make black women "clinical," to use his words. Here is how he described his last sexual experience with a black woman:

> *"Ouch! I'm hot. I always get hot. Cut on the fan. I'm dry. I don't want to do it in this position no more," she said. Then after about fifteen minutes of touching and licking and touching and intercourse, I was done. And she was okay with everything.*

How is it that black women could go from this historical image of explosive black sexuality to being seen as sexual prudes? The answer, in part, is by comparison! Compare Derrick's last sexual experience with a black woman to his last sexual experience with a woman in Brazil:

> *They were obedient—not like they were afraid I was going to whip them, but open to anything. She was open. She was initiating things sexually. I didn't have to convince her to do anything. And when she was going down, I could tell that she was enjoying it. She was hooking a brother up—licking my balls, licking my ass. The sex was wild. It was just incredible. There was no humiliation. There was no detachment.*

When black men come back from Brazil, by far one of the biggest complaints that they have is about the restrictive sexuality of black women. Inspired by the explosive and exploratory sexual experiences overseas, they are able to see more clearly what they have been lacking sexually in the States. As a result, the sexual hierarchy switches from "once you go black, you'll never go back" to "once you go to Brazil, you'll have to go back again."

Men literally ask themselves the questions that Derrick raised: "If I didn't have sex with Brazilian women, would I be able to recognize a sexual woman? Would I think sex was just about bumping and grinding and ejaculating and that's it?"

In the end, the sexual activities that black women tend not to engage in, as well as their overall attitudes about sex and sexuality, become a major source of concern and criticism. And in comparison to Brazilian women, black women are downright frigid.

Is Receiving Better than Giving: Sexual Mismatches

For Derrick and men like him, Brazil simply confirms something they already thought: that black women are sexually inhibited. Black women simply don't engage in the types of sexual activities that other women do. From his perspective, black women's attitudes toward sex show a selfishness and lack of confidence to explore their sexuality fully.

The research that has been done on sexual acts and attitudes in general show that there are no major differences between blacks, whites, and other groups in terms of what they do between the sheets or what they think about doing between the sheets. There are no major differences between racial and ethnic groups in terms of how they get their freak on. The research also shows that what major differences do exist in attitudes, beliefs, and behaviors are generally differences between men and women across racial lines. However, within these broad distinctions, the researchers do find important differences between black men and women in both the sexual acts that they participate in and their attitudes toward sexuality.

The most glaring differences that researchers typically find are around fellatio, or what Derrick jokingly referred to as black women's inability to speak into the microphone. Based on the best data available, the research shows that black women were the least likely of all women to engage in oral sex. According to the most recent data, compared to Hispanic women, black women were barely half as likely to have participated in active oral sex in their lifetime, and a third as likely to have participated in active oral sex compared to white women. Similarly, black men were the least likely of all men to report participating in active oral sex compared with either white or Hispanic men.

So if black men and women are both lowest on fellatio, maybe it is because both groups don't enjoy it. Nothing can be further from the truth if you ask men. In fact, reports show that black males like fellatio "somewhat *more* than other men." The reason given for why the rates are so low is because black women think it is disgusting. From Derrick's perspective, the selfish part is that they don't mind oral sex being performed on them. Derrick believes that how a woman relates to his penis says a lot about her sexuality but also a lot about men. According to him, a man's penis is special and that men enjoy having it treated as if it's special and enjoyed.

In addition to the oral sex issue, there is another area of difference that seems to separate black men and women: anal sex. An article in the *New Yorker* magazine titled "Anal-sex talk still makes people blush" talked about the rise in popularity of anal sex among heterosexuals. It reported,

> *Centers for Disease Control's National Survey of Family Growth, it's rapidly becoming a regular feature of hetero couples' horizontal activities. The survey, released last year, showed that 38.2 percent of men between twenty and thirty-nine and 32.6 percent of women ages eighteen to forty-four engage in heterosexual anal sex. Compare that with the CDC's 1992 National Health and Social Life survey, which found that only 25.6 percent of men eighteen to fifty-nine and 20.4 percent of women eighteen to fifty-nine indulged in it.*

The article didn't go into racial breakdowns. However, the research that has been done on the percentages of people who engage in anal sex does show important differences between racial and ethnic groups and between men and women. Similar to the research on oral sex, the research shows that both black women and black men were the least likely to participate in anal sex. In fact, white women (23 percent) and Hispanic women (19 percent) were twice as likely to have participated in anal sex in their lifetime compared to black women (10 percent). In contrast, black men were only slightly less likely to have participated in anal sex in their lifetime.

These differences in sexual practices are presumably what causes disagreement between professional black men and women. It is also these differences or sexual mismatches that cause black men to pursue other options, according to Jordan, a mortgage broker from New York:

If you're not sucking dick, taking it up the ass, letting me squirt on the face, or doing whatever it is I want you to do, I don't want to be with you. I don't necessarily want to do all of that, but I want the option. I don't need my women to do a threesome, but I don't want her to tell me no. I want her to say, "I'll think about it."

I find a lot of black women are dream busters. They shoot down your dreams sexually. You want to watch porn and they say it's nasty. So you sneak and watch porn by yourself, and jerk off by yourself, rather than doing it with your woman. That's why I never got married after my divorce. I don't need a woman to contribute to my rent. I don't need a financial

partner; I got my own money. I don't need a woman to vali-
date my intelligence. I'm not interested in her degrees.

I need a woman who will [allow me to express myself]
sexually. I wouldn't consider her a freak; I would consider her
adventurous—that she would try something new, that if I had
a dream or a fantasy that was outlandish, that she wouldn't
bust my dreams. But a lot of these women are dream busters.

What Jordan is saying is what a lot of professional men want to say. They don't need a woman for money or even her intellect. They don't require black women in areas that affirm them economically or intellectually. Rather, what professional men need are women to affirm them in areas that are social and sexual in nature. In many ways, it is very similar to the idea of a "maintenance man." But in this instance, it's more like a "sustenance woman."

Middle-class and professional black men don't just want or need something to tide them over; what they want or need are women who cater to their sexual needs. In order to do that, the woman has to be in touch with her own sexuality. They have to have an attitude that doesn't interfere with the sexual act.

Derrick consistently referred to black women's negative attitude toward sex. He said that black women have such detachment, insecurity, and often shame associated with their sexuality that the experience is not enjoyable. He actually attributes this to the idea that they hate black men.

Brazil: The Ultimate Freaknik

The dominant belief among men who travel to Brazil is that American women in general, and black women in particular, are inhibited sexually compared to Brazilian women. And they argue that their perspective is not restricted to their experience with Brazilian prostitutes. Instead, they argue that the main difference in sexuality is based on culture differences and not "pay for play." Here is what David, in Fort Lauderdale, said:

> *We live in the United States, which is an extremely repressive society. And for people to get outside of our society for a moment to see what it is like to feel a little freedom from the moral repression of the United States is just exhilarating! This Judeo-Christian ethic legislates your morality. The trouble is that we are so good at it that we don't know we're repressed, not until you see something else and then you say, "Wow!"*
>
> *These (Brazilians) are wild. They are not wild actually; they are normal. America is a country full of symbols and games. They hide your sexuality under the rug. All we do is talk about, "this is wrong" and "that is wrong." Why are these things wrong? Because of the Bible? We have a lot of laws and rules that are moral in nature—from blue laws to what age is legal. If a ninety-one-year-old guy fucks an eighteen-year-old girl, there is nothing wrong with that. But if an eighteen-year-old guy fucks a sixteen-year-old girl, that's rape.*

The suggestion that the United States is a place of moral repression that leads to sexual inhibitions is widely popular.

It's something that men presumably don't see in other countries, particularly Brazil. What ends up happening is, these men develop a belief that Brazilian women are more open to sexual acts than women in the States.

A survey on the incidence of anal and oral sex in Brazil reported that at least occasionally, 52.9 percent of Brazilians have practiced anal intercourse. That is more than twice the overall rate reported in the U.S. and more than four times the rate of black women. According to reports, this is due to Brazilian culture's emphasis on *fazendo tudo*, *tesão* (excitement), and *prazer* (enjoyment). This promotes "rather elaborate and varied forms of sexual foreplay," a strong emphasis on oral sex, and especially a focus on anal sex.

The ultimate example that men use to demonstrate the cultural embrace of sex and sexuality in Brazil is Carnival. Unlike Freaknik or BET's *Spring Bling*, Carnival is not considered an aberration of "Girls Gone Wild" or college students being involved in a sexual break. Rather, Carnival draws millions of people and is considered an adult event that characterizes the cultural embrace of sexuality. Here is a description of Carnival listed in *The Encyclopedia of Sexuality*:

> *. . . an erotic universe focused on the transgression of public norms through a playfulness reminiscent of . . . one's adolescent sexual experience and the excitations they produced play[ing] themselves out again repeatedly throughout adult life. They undercut the effects of sexual prohibitions and make polymorphous pleasures such as oral and anal intercourse, an important part even of married, heterosexual relationships. Such acts*

[whether engaged in with same- or other-gendered persons, a nonspouse, or a stranger], along with the tesão or excitement which is thought to underlie them and the prazer or enjoyment which is understood to be their aim, are essential to the Brazilian sexual culture, with its context of "no shame," "within four walls," "beneath the sheets," or "behind the mask."

When black men travel to Carnival, they don't see young people involved in immature sexual behavior. They see a cultural tradition and a sense of pride in the participants that they equate with sexual liberation. So when they come back, they show pictures, videos, and PowerPoint presentations to all who will listen, to show how free Brazil is—not just in its racial attitudes but in its *sexual* attitudes.

So the big difference between Brazilian women and black American women is in their attitudes toward sex, not in the sex act itself. Brazilian women are seen as enjoying and participating in sex in ways that please not only their partners but also themselves. And this attitude isn't found just in the prostitutes—it is cultural. Brazil becomes this place that is progressive for black people. Moreover, Brazil is seen as this progressive place for black *men*.

Professional Black Women and the "Big O"

One of the paradoxes found in research is that married black women report poorer health than unmarried black women. This finding demands more understanding of what actually happens within black marriages to explain this phenomenon.

Another paradox found in research is that middle-class black women were least likely to say that they were satisfied sexually. According to sociologist Orlando Patterson, middle-class black women were behind both middle-class white women and middle-class Hispanic women in finding sex physically satisfying. In addition, middle-class black women were the group least inclined to say that they were "very" or "extremely satisfied" emotionally with their sex lives.

Why do middle-class black women have such problems with sexual satisfaction, physically and mentally? If you ask men, it is their attitudes and insecurities. If you ask some men, they will say it has to do with their involvement in the church. Here is what one man said:

A lot of professional women are involved in the church. According to my church, if you want to have sex with someone, that's considered lust and adultery. And if you want to have sex outside of "normal," or standard sex, you are really sinning. So even if you're my wife and I want to role-play or have oral or anal sex, that comes under the list of sinning. I know a lot of women who believe that and look down on anything outside of standard sex.

So it's not "What's love got to do with it?" but rather "What's *religion* got to do with it?" And while there are countless books currently available about spirituality and sexuality, men who travel to Brazil are quick to point out that America is no more "Christian" a nation than Brazil.

"It's kind of odd that we would call ourselves a Christian nation, although if you go to Latin America, all of those women are Christian," said Sam, who travels to Brazil twice a year. "In Latin America, Catholicism is the fastest-growing religion. We place moral values and a moral code on our lives. If a woman sleeps around, she's not a woman, whereas [in Brazil] a woman is not any less of a human being."

Invariably, it comes back to what women are willing to do. This begs the question, what, then, do professional black men want of black women sexually? Sam said what professional black men want is a "sophistislut."

"We want a sophisticated woman who is a slut," he said. "We want a woman who can go into the boardroom and handle herself with her business suit but can also wear a miniskirt and a thong, showing just enough cleavage with some heels with an ankle strap, and then can come home and take care of her man."

Returning to Derrick, his explanation again is that he needs a black woman who is open and free with their sexuality.

I have to have a woman who is in tune with her sexuality, who doesn't have any shame, who is in tune with herself, who is comfortable with herself. I want a woman who is open. If I can get that, I don't need to be screwing thirteen and fourteen women.

Conclusion: Neither Freaky nor Frigid

Black women are not freaks. Contrary to whatever ideas may exist in the white imagination, it is the white woman who actually has the highest number of sexual partners (fifteen or more male sexual partners). That's more than the average black woman and twice as many as Hispanic women.

Black women are not frigid, either. Contrary to this new counterimage developing from men who travel overseas, black women are not a restricted group sexually. Black women do tend to be more traditional in their attitudes toward sex and less recreational compared to other groups. While they have fewer sexual partners than white women, they report similar numbers of male sexual partners in their lifetime compared to women of other races. What black women tend to be is *faithful* in their relationships—despite not being as physically and emotionally satisfied as other groups of women.

When you consider that middle-class and professional black men report high rates of physical satisfaction with their primary sexual partners, while at the same time reporting a high rate of infidelity, you begin to see that the problem is *not* with the black woman but with the black *man*.

How is it that men report being satisfied but still seek out outside relationships? The answer is that black men are able to participate in their own construction of sexuality. They are able to construct their sexuality, black women's sexuality, and certainly the sexuality of Brazilian women. Sam, thirty-two-years-old, provides a good example of this when describing the sexuality of a black professional woman he was recently involved with:

> *I started dating this woman around Thanksgiving. For four or five months we didn't have sex. She was just prudish. I mean, I was with her for four or five months and didn't get the pussy. She used all kinds of different rationale. She said she*

was setting an example for her teenage son, who lived with her, by not having men staying the night. But then she didn't really want to come over to my place and stay, because she couldn't leave her son alone. She said that one man she dated, she met him at a hotel, but that she felt cheap doing that.

She pretty much had a system set up to keep it from happening. She didn't want to have sex, but she wanted to be exclusive. I said to her, "So you want a committed, noncommitted relationship?"

I couldn't wait to get to Rio. As soon as I stepped off the plane, I got me some—and with this gorgeous girl, too. I didn't even know the girl. I just pulled her out of a club. I had to.

In this example, what ends up being considered prudish behavior was more an attitude toward sexuality in light of this woman's circumstances. Because this woman wanted to be a role model for her son, and because she didn't want to feel degraded by meeting in hotels, she was considered a prude. *But not the Brazilian women.*

The larger issue embedded here is that men fail to consider how the issue of shame and detachment that black women may experience may come from men's behavior and not the women's sexual inhibitions. If black women feel that they are required or forced to participate in sex acts because they might lose their man, how does that make them feel? If they feel less into sex because, in the back of their mind, they have good evidence that their man is cheating, how should they feel? If a black woman tells her man that certain sex acts are demeaning and defiling, then she's a "dream buster."

There are some obvious and not so obvious questions here. One obvious question is, how is it that one's desires automatically take precedence over another's desires in a relationship? Why does a black man's perspective on sex take precedence over a black woman's? But a not-so-obvious question is, when did middle-class and professional black men become so independent of women? When did that independence day occur? Was it a moment? Did it come with a certificate of graduation or achievement?

The point is that so much of the independence that middle-class and professional men speak of is based on the idea that they need women only in certain ways. The problem is that this image lacks a memory, thus omitting all the things that got them there. Black women have struggled and sacrificed at every level so that black people could benefit from their current accomplishments. And for men to deny that history is sort of like a person benefiting from the movement that produced affirmative action, then later saying that they did it all on their own.

There is a critique that the United States is a morally repressed society. You could feel like a right-wing radical Republican while arguing for a type of sexual conservatism that leads to responsible and safe sexual choices. That is part of the trap of talking about anything less than sexual freedom as "conservative." However, you don't have to be a conservative Christian or a fundamentalist Muslim to know that who you share your body with and how you share your body is possibly one of the most political things you can do. So-called liberals and progressives have a responsibility to talk to young men about sex and sexuality and remove the myth that "free love" means putting your penis anywhere, anytime, with anybody.

The United States is politically repressive, and it is incumbent on black men to have the same sort of passion that they demonstrate for sexual freedom and apply it to the pursuit of other freedoms. The black and brown community is in desperate need of leadership with integrity, and it is difficult to see how bedding ten to twelve women will inspire the type of leadership with integrity that we long for.

Chapter Seven

Fat, Black, and Ugly: Size _Does_ Matter!

A man's self-esteem is tied to having a beautiful woman by his side. That says that I am the man. But when you're walking down the street and you have Big Bertha on your arm, that says, "This is all I can get."

My first wife got bigger and bigger after our first child, and she became obese after our second child. She is a sweetheart. But after a while she wasn't physically appealing to me. The more she gained weight, especially after our second child, the less attractive she was to me. Then came the whole issue of getting an erection, which was getting harder and harder for me to achieve. And her size started to matter more and more. My own self-esteem started to suffer with her weight issue.

As my ex-wife started to gain weight, I started to focus on other things—like her boobs. Her boobs got bigger and that was exciting. But of course, as her boobs got bigger, so did everything else. And that started to affect me sexually. A male's penis is only so big. My friend used to say that being with an overweight woman was intimidating with their really big be-

hinds. When you put that penis against a really big butt, your penis gets intimidated, it looks so small. That definitely affects your arousal level. A woman with a smaller frame makes you feel like you can break her in two and dominate her sexually. You don't feel as dominant when a woman's size challenges your own. So you only do the missionary position.

Nobody wants to have a sexual partner that they can only do one position with. Okay, we can do it missionary style, and psychologically I'm okay because I can see her pretty face. But I want to switch it up every now and then. If we were to have more children, I would have done a lot of things to stay in the relationship. But I would have probably have had a pretty young, thin thing on the side, too. I'm just keeping it real.

The higher you go up the ladder [of success], the less weight you are allowed to have. It's certainly true in my professional life. The whole weight issue has been put out by inner-city, urban brothers. Look at our culture. What goes on in the hood permeates the rest of black society. Black people pattern ourselves after what happens in the hood, and what the thug brothers did for us was set this standard that they wanted women to be thick. And we see that played out in videos. The portrayal of the sister was that she was attractive if she had junk in the trunk. And there is a cost to having junk in the trunk. If you have a big butt, you're more likely to have a big everything else. And there's a thin line between thick and obese.

I work with a lot of professional black women, and a lot of them are overweight. I hate to put a social stigma on it, but you really don't find very attractive successful black women. You don't find that a lot. I have seen a lot of women who are successful, but physically and visually, they are not exactly stunning. My preference now is for a slender woman.

—Stanley, 37, a Realtor from Philadelphia

Stanley's view is significant because even though he sometimes made light of the situation (pun intended), it was clear that he had done some thinking about how a woman's size, particularly his ex-wife's, affected his sexuality and his overall stature and self-esteem as a professional man. His ultimate decision to date only slender women suggests that he has not thought enough or doesn't care enough about how this weight issue affects black women. The problem for Stanley and other men who travel to Brazil and other countries in search of "the perfect woman" is that black women's weight has become an issue that men bring back from their experiences with Brazilian women.

So in addition to coming back with a new sexual standard by which they judge and compare black women, they also come back with a new *physical* standard by which they judge and compare black women. This is something that Jermaine, in Memphis, can attest to:

If I could create a woman, the Brazilian woman would be it. They are all about five feet six or small, they have that "good" hair with the light tan complexion or the bronze skin. They

do have some darker ones, but not a lot. To m
sisters . . . or at least what sisters used to look
look like.

Today, the average sister is a size sixteen.
much bigger than a size six in Brazil, no matter what age.
They could be in their fifties and they might be a size eight,
but they don't get much bigger than that. You can't even find
a size ten or twelve in the stores there. And they all have nice,
round booties—just like sisters. But the sisters have gotten so
big now that their booties are too big. (I never thought I would
say that, but your booty can be too big!)

The disdain for the size of black women in America is often articulated subtly in the forms of jokes and innuendo, which even the random white person can occasionally pick up on, as reflected on ESPN's Bill Simmon's sports blog:

I watch those House of Payne *commercials and feel constantly confused. What about the part when he's trying to work the remote and his gigantic wife asks what he's doing and he says angrily, "I'm trying to turn you into Beyonce." That was the funniest clip they could pull for the commercial? I don't get it. That seems like an angry, unhappy show to me. And can anyone figure out the whole "comic dressing up in drag as multiple characters" thing? Why is this funny? I'm so confused by* House of Payne. *It makes me feel sad every time they show the ad. Which is every three minutes.*

You can't turn on the television or go to a movie and not see contempt for black women play out—from the Pine-Sol ommercial with the fat, black sassy woman shaking her finger at people to keep their homes clean to *House of Payne*, to Tyler Perry, Martin Lawrence, and Eddie Murphy perpetuating and solidifying the image of the fat, loud, rude, black woman in the many *Madea* chronicles, the *Big Momma* movies, and *Norbert*.

While America laughs, the image of black women is indelibly etched in the minds of everyone. It goes back as far as Mammy and Aunt Jemima, and it's still prevalent today.

It's no laughing matter. There is even a club in New York City, called the Harlem Club, which bans fat black women from its membership. According to the founder of this proposed elite black men's social club, his gentlemen members deserve the best.

"When people think of the Harlem Club, I want them to think beautiful, intelligent, highly successful women of color," said founder Thomas Lopez-Pierre. "So to accomplish this, there would be strict membership guidelines for the club."

Here is a sample of the guidelines:

Women could join the Harlem Club, too. But only as "associate" members. And they had to be thirty-five or younger, unmarried, childless, college educated and willing to submit a head-to-toe photograph, to prevent unattractive women from making the cut.

To emphasize this point, the founder, Mr. Lopez-Pierre, said that at the time of this book, more than five hundred women had applied and that he had "deleted the e-mail applications of overweight women."

What's interesting about this attempt at paradise is that despite the bravado behind such decisions, there was never any detailed explanation offered or required as to why the men had such preferences.

But what's "attractive"? Individual choices or tastes vary. But what's clear is that fat, or overweight, is definitely not attractive. The Harlem Club is a perfect metaphor for how some professional black men understand and try to deal with black women's weight—by controlling black women and blaming or containing poor black men. So black women's size is not just an issue for black men in general but for professional black men in particular.

There is a health aspect to consider. And if these men wanted to take the approach that they love their women and they want to see them live long, vibrant lives, that may be a welcome approach to deal with the obesity of many of our sisters. But for these men, this is not the case.

The reality is that weight is a problem among black women—a real health problem that is well documented and in fact becoming worse: In 1998 the average black woman wore a size 18, but today she wears size 20. According to published reports, black women are twice as obese as white women. And the proportion of black women who are obese is eighty percent higher than that of black men. In addition, obesity is linked to diabetes as a major cause of morbidity and mortality in the United States. Consequently, cities with large

African-American populations, such as Cleveland and Detroit, have high rates of obesity and diabetes.

Keith, a business owner from Atlanta, was able to articulate
what some men feel when looking at an overweight woman:

*There used to be a time when a black woman had nice propor-
tions, and you called her "thick." Now you got black women
who are size eighteen talking about "I'm thick." Now, baby,
you done passed thick about three sizes ago. I can't even pick
you up and I'm not even trying.*

*I think everybody wants to be with someone who cares
enough about themselves to take care of themselves. For me,
personally, when I look at a woman that has just really let
herself go, who allowed herself to get out of control, I think that
I could be potentially signing up for a lot of health problems
down the road. Who wants that burden?*

While Keith seems concerned about the health of overweight women, I think Stanley's and Thomas Lopez-Pierre's
views are more common. They are more accurate in explaining
why many black men—especially professional black men—
have such disdain for overweight women. Stanley makes the
important point about how a woman's size affects him sexually, in terms of his personal interests and appetites, but also
socially, in terms of his sense of self-worth and his own status
and prestige as man and as a professional.

These are essentially the two main issues that men have
with black women's weight: (1) that a woman's size is filtered
thorough the cultural lens of what is sexually exciting; and

(2) what it means in terms of their social stature as men and as professionals.

Stanley shows how both these issues are intimately connected with his own sense of self-worth.

Big Black Women and the Dominatrix

The relationship between men's sexual interests and appetites and women's weight is something that many men who have traveled to Brazil talk about upon returning. It's as if, by having a point of reference, they could see more clearly what their overall sexual experience was like, as communicated by Deon, from Pittsburgh:

> When I have gotten with Brazilian women, the more attractive, the more physically fit, the more I am willing to go that extra mile. But if you're average, then I am more likely to think about how quickly can I get it done. When you tie it all down, it comes back to looks.

To the extent that weight does factor into men's sexuality in terms of their interest and excitement, it is really a portal into men's social and emotional experience. If you listen to Stanley, you recognize that a man's interests are mediated through the lens of domination and his ability to perform. When he and his friends refer to women with big butts, jokingly or not, as "intimidating," what they are addressing specifically is a form of performance anxiety. Typically, when we think of performance anxiety, we think of an individual sexual problem that confronts men in a sexual situation. We don't think of performance anxiety as a sexual problem that is applied to an entire group of women.

However, this is exactly what Stanley was referring to when he talked about being intimidated by big-butted and big-bodied women. It's what Lil' Kim meant when she talked about how she used to be "scared of the dick." For Stanley, the individual problem is applied to an entire category of women when he decides to avoid big women. The important thing is that he is able to identify portions of why this was the case. And he was able to acknowledge, in a small way, the role of domination as a part of his own sexuality and how this affects his sexual interest and his ability to perform.

When we hear about sex and domination, we tend to think of one or two things. The first thing we think about is whips and chains, handcuffs, leather—things that typically fall under the category of BDSM (bondage, discipline, submission, and domination). We associate these kinds of sexual practices with so-called freaky people. There was a comedian who joked about a woman handcuffing him during sex: "Now I know how it feels to be handcuffed. And trust me, there ain't nothing sexy in that!"

The second thing we think about when we consider sex and domination is rape and other forms of abuse. However, domination is much more generally a part of men's sexuality than we acknowledge. According to research, it influences not only men's pleasure but also the personal choices that men make about whom to have sex with, in addition to the type of sex they have. In fact, research consistently shows that men link dominance and power with sexual pleasure more than women do—not that most men are rapists, nor are the majority involved in explicit forms of S and M. Most men are intimately affected by feelings of dominance in sexual situations and this affects their attitudes and behaviors toward women.

What this means for Stanley is that a woman's size becomes a benchmark for him sexually. It's a marker for what he can and can't do in sexual situations—and not just in terms of physical positions, as he hinted at. Even when Stanley referred to how weight affected his choice of sexual positions, it was less that he felt limited, and more that he felt inadequate. It had to do with his anxieties, insecurities, and perspectives on sex. So, to the extent that he and other men want to feel dominant in sex, avoiding bigger women will always be a part of their personal choices because big women make them feel small. Instead of being honest, most men prefer to degrade the women instead of saying, "Yes, your size does matter, but it matters because it makes me feel weak and ineffectual."

It's easier to focus on women's large size and talk about it as if it were a health problem that most concerned them. A woman's size and weight may factor into a man's sexuality, but not always in ways that are apparent. Men may be more concerned with their performance, which gets projected onto women. In fact, it has nothing to do with women. Size matters sexually, but not necessarily physically. It is what black women's physical makeup represents to men and their self-esteem and sense of self-worth that matters most.

For Stanley, his sense of self-worth was deeply connected with his image of social class. Not only were big women intimidating sexually in terms of his performance, they were also intimidating socially and in the workplace. Stanley mentioned having a "Big Bertha" by his side and told the world this was all he could get, suggesting he was a failure as a man—particularly as a professional man. The idea that overweight black women do not fit within the professional world is something that many men talked about.

Keith explained it this way:

Size is huge. That's why these ultrasuccessful guys have this trophy wife. Part of your status in the world as a man is the woman that's on your arm. This is true whether people want to talk about it or not. Can a brother have a trophy wife that's big? She'd be a roomful of trophies.

Keith goes on to argue that there is really no excuse for black women to be overweight or obese, because of what he sees professional, white women being able to accomplish:

In corporate America, I work with a lot of women—white women, who have two and three kids. And they are gorgeous. They're in shape. I'm not a woman, so I don't know all the changes that they go through when they have a child. But when I see these white women every day who have kids who manage to work out and take care of themselves . . . They manage to keep their hair done, looking nice, smelling good.

Those white women are up in the morning and hitting the gym before they do something, because they still believe in being active. They're not saying," I can't because I have kids." Part of the problem with black women is that a lot of them are

*in a relationship and they don't have help to take care of those
kids. A white woman may have a nanny or something, so I'll
give them that. But I know a lot of brothers with white girls
because the girls look good. That's it. It's not that they prefer them more than black women. They just prefer a woman
who's in shape over the woman who isn't.*

What he is essentially arguing is that there is no excuse
for a black woman to be fat, because white women are able
to keep off the weight, even when they have children. This
is one of the reasons why black men choose white women:
because they are healthy and in shape—not because they are
white. What is crucially important to notice is how the explanation shifts from Stanley blaming poor black men for the
size of black women to Keith justifying why black men choose
white women.

What Stanley mentioned earlier about how poor or inner-
city black men set the cultural standards for black life is not an
unimportant acknowledgment for professional men. It suggests that not only elite white men are in charge of setting the
standards for black women—so are poor black men. When
you combine that with Keith's idea that brothers reluctantly
choose white women, then you can understand why professional black men seek to set strict guidelines about the size
of black women—because every other group of men seems to
have control, except for them.

The larger issue for professional black men like Stanley
and Jeremy is the requirement that they fit into the business
and corporate class. Intuitively, we know what the research

consistently confirms about the realities of work and career advancement. To be successful, one has to have a certain amount of credentials. And you have to have access; you have to be able to network. The age-old adage that it's not what you know but who you know applies here. But for black folks, what you know still matters a lot.

To be truly successful, blacks also know that they need the added skill of being able to fit in. Whether it is dressing a certain way, talking a certain way, or laughing a certain way that allows people to feel comfortable, being able to conform to the social settings that black professionals find themselves in is important. For professional black men, that may mean knowing what suits to wear, the proper way to tie their tie, what cuff links or briefcase are appropriate, how to order from a menu, and so on. All these are attributes that give a person the ability to interact in elite social settings.

In addition to all this, a professional man is also judged by the woman he has by his side. Men have trophy wives as "visible and seductive symbols" of their success and masculinity. Trophy wives are not only educated and sophisticated, but also small or slender, to use Stanley's language. The size of the woman by his side is important.

Professional black men are judged by their ability to replicate standards of success even when it comes to women. The point is not that professional black men develop a "taste" for slender women the same way they do for balsamic vinaigrette—well, maybe some do—more important, whether they like it or not, the size of their spouse gives them access to elite white worlds where big women, black or white, are not welcome.

Even if a professional black man is capable of successfully navigating between worlds, it is not easy to switch a black woman's size. It becomes incumbent on him to choose a woman who fits that corporate image, or to be vigilant about making sure that she stays under the weight requirement. Here is how Lisa, a black woman with two master's degrees working in banking in Chicago, described the painful way that weight played out in her relationship:

My husband made six digits, so he brought with him a white value system of beauty. Because I had a black body and then had gained weight, he was totally turned off in the bedroom. There was no loving. I didn't look the way he wanted me to look. What he really wanted was a white woman with black skin.

Six-digit men are not typically going to get a big woman. They buy into that white value system, that white culture. Typically, in corporate America if they're going to climb the ladder, there's a certain look that goes along with that. I'm not that look. Yes, color-wise I was perfect. I even had perfect hair. But I got heavy and that wasn't appropriate, and he got turned off.

One time we were in the midst of having sex, and he got up and said, "I can't do this. I don't find you attractive." Another time we were on an airplane, going on a belated honeymoon that we never got a chance to take, and his boss happened to be on the same plane. I had just had our second child and had gained weight. He wouldn't introduce me to his boss. Finally, his boss got up and said, "How are you?" He spoke and still didn't introduce me. His boss had to say, "Is this your wife?" My husband didn't say anything. I had to raise my hand and say, "Yes," and introduce myself because my husband was too embarrassed.

Brazilian women don't have to worry about weight issues, because they make staying in shape a priority. Looks are important to Brazilian women. According to Tank in Louisville,

There are a lot of sisters getting too big, and I'm talking about women over thirty, which means that it's probably going to get worse for them. They get one kid and blow up. It's not a matter of aging; it's a matter of taking care of yourself—doing those things that are important.

Brazilian women aren't used to buying everything they want. Even women who make a moderate income seem to live very well within their means. They discipline themselves. Brazilian women don't spend all that they make so that they're not always under the stress of trying to get out there and beat down that dollar, where they have the time to take care of themselves. They're also not eating the foods that make them blow up. They do everything in moderation so they keep their bodies together, whereas sister, man, seem to be eating everything!

Unlike either black women or white women, Brazilian women don't need to work out. They don't need a Nordic Track, because they have to trek to the market. They get their exercise just going through their everyday lives. And they practically live on the beaches. For them, beauty and staying in shape is not something they have to worry about—it's a way of life.

Brazilian Women: Halle Berry on Steroids

One man's testament would not be enough to capture how often men talk about the beauty of Brazilian women. Without exception, the most consistent thing mentioned in conversations was the beauty of Brazilian women: "drop-dead gorgeous," "more beautiful than you could ever imagine," "absolutely spectacular," "bath water-drinking fine." Those are just a few tributes bestowed on Brazilian women by the men I talked with. As one man plainly put it, "Brazilian women are the most beautiful women I have ever seen!"

Another explained, "No one prepared me. There are no words that can capture what these women were like. Literally, the moment I got off of the airplane and stepped into the baggage claim area, I saw some of the most beautiful women I had ever seen. And it just got better from there."

To communicate how attractive Brazilian women are, men often refer to scales. One lawyer stated that, "there were no sevens and eights. If there were thirty women, twenty-five of them were tens and five were twelves."

His friend, a fellow attorney, agreed, saying, "Even a cute girl was a ten by our standards."

Another way the men communicated the beauty of Brazilian women was to compare their looks to popular stars.

One financial analyst said, "All of these women were Jennifer Lopez, Halle Berry, and women in the Snoop Dogg videos." Another attribute men highlighted was the diversity of the Brazilian women.

"There were blondes with white skin, Spanish-looking women, to black Africans with jet-black skin," one stockbroker pointed out.

Virtually every man talked about being "blown away," not just by the beauty of the Brazilian women but also by how *many* beautiful women there were. The consensus was that you could find some black women in the States who looked like this, but not in the numbers that you could find in Rio. Ralph explained the difference between women in the States and women in Rio:

I hate to say it, but American women let themselves go. They have children as they've gotten older; they're not in the gym; they're not concerned about working out; they don't necessarily keep their hair and stuff up to par.

If you want to compare that to the Brazilian women, not all of them but the ones that people have interacted with in that Copacabana triangle, in that area, they're working out. They already have that natural, wavy hair. They have the green eyes because of the melting pot of people there.

I think men get confused when they see these beautiful, model-type women who are everyday in Brazil, and they want to try to compare that to what's back home—wherever their home may be. The reality is that it's just not the reality in the states. In Rio, I was going with this fine woman who was five feet five with an hourglass figure, with hair down the middle of her back. She was just gorgeous. You're not going to find too many like that in America. Number one, there are no beaches. The best I can hope for is a woman who is five two, who doesn't go to the gym.

Overall, there is so much reverence given to the beauty of Brazilian women and the sheer number of beautiful women that it borders on a form of mysticism. Here is how one travel agency described the beach scene in Rio:

Watch and enjoy the ritual that Carioca women go through when they enter the water. It is almost always the same, truly amazing, learned from childhood, a flick of the hair, and adjusting of the bikini top, a quick dunk, another flip of the hair, adjustment of the top and bottom, back to their tanga, and combing of the hair, always while standing up . . .

—*Travel Guide*

Everything about Brazilian women is beautiful—from the way they walk to the way they smell, even to the way they bathe. Why are they so beautiful? Because they are the product of a sixteenth- and seventeenth-century historical chemistry experiment in which African, Portuguese, and native blood were mixed. The end result was this product that men commonly referred to as Halle Berry on steroids.

In contrast, blacks in general, and black women in particular, have been portrayed as the opposite of the white standard of beauty. With the image of big lips, short nappy-woolly hair, big, broad noses, black women have been portrayed as the antithesis of white female beauty. We all grew up hearing the saying "If you're white, you're all right. If you're brown, you can stick around. But if you're black, step back."

This type of "pigmentocracy," in which the closer you are to white, the more beautiful you are, is well known. In the past, if black men had to choose between black and white, there was no way that black women could compare with the white standard of skin tone or hair texture and length. But with tan, bronze, or olive skin, black men don't have to choose; they can have both. Brazilian women are the real deal. Brazilian women are not just black Barbies—white but colored black. They are not carbon copies of white women. They have long hair naturally, fair skin naturally, colored eyes naturally. And perhaps the most important thing that brothers have always coveted: they have the onion, the bubble, the butt, the behind, of a sister.

Black Booty versus Brazilian *Bundas*

It is actually difficult to put into words how popular and significant the Brazilian behind, or what is referred to as a *"bunda,"* is in the minds and imaginations of men around the world—especially black men. The Brazilian *bunda* is not flat like white women's, and it is not large like black women's. It is not too big and definitely not too small. It is round and plump, but the body attached to it isn't. It is considered the perfect butt. It has become the "gold standard" for measuring butts. Here is how the Web site Brazilianbundas.com described what makes Brazilian *bundas* so special:

African blood gives the full roundness and the Native Brazil-
ian heritage, which gives the women the long thin waistline
that makes the bunda appear even larger.

Historically, there has never been a time when "other"
women could compete with black women physically. In fact,
the constant critique against white women was that they had
pale skin and did not have hips, breasts, and certainly not
the ass of black women. Sisters could always take some comfort knowing that despite how the white woman was set up
as the standard for beauty in America, white women really
couldn't compete with the assets that sisters possessed. White
women would routinely do everything from tanning to getting collagen injections in their lips to butt implants to make
themselves more beautiful (or look more like black women).
Sisters were the ultimate brick house. That has all changed
with Brazilian women.

Brazilian butts are so popular that Brazilian butt augmen-
tations are becoming one of the most popular forms of cos-
metic surgery. Today, the butt that white girls covet is the
Brazilian butt, not the ghetto booty. Brazilian butt augmenta-
tion is only now catching up to the popularity of the Brazilian hair wax. _Desperate Housewives_ Eva Longoria reportedly
bragged, "Every girl should have a Brazilian wax. It's my sexy
secret. And I only wear thongs. I don't own a pair of knickers
with a proper back to them."

Everything that is physically Brazilian is coded as beautiful
or the standard. Today Brazilian women's butts have become
the signature sign of their beauty and physical superiority,

while at the same time, black women's butts have become the metaphor for overweight, out of shape, and lack of care. In essence, the black woman's butt is the embodiment of all that is wrong with a woman today.

The fixation on the butt is part of an objectification of women that has to be resisted and not celebrated. It continues the focus on parts and not people. The question for men is, when they look at women can they actually see the *woman*? I was in a popular Brazilian chat room and was stung by some of the comments on its message board. I could only imagine how much pain those attitudes have caused black women.

It was the comments of one woman in particular that stood out for me. She was a black woman, and she knew that her husband had been traveling to Brazil with a group of friends, but she didn't think anything of it until she discovered that he was staying in contact with this community online. She read some of his e-mail and discovered the truth. She outed him on this message board in this Brazilian chat room.

But it was the way the men responded to her that told the tale. They attacked this woman, calling her fat and questioning how big her butt was and saying that's probably why her husband was going to Rio and why he would probably continue going and that she wasn't woman enough to stop it. The barrage was brutal and hostile.

Conclusion: Dream Girls and the Black Male Minstrels

If you even talk to African-American women, they're intimidated about how these Brazilian women look. Intimi-

dated. And that goes for my own experience. There is such fear.

—Michael

The film *Dreamgirls* is the story of a group of black female singers who were able to achieve success despite the many challenges they faced on their way to the top. On one hand it is a triumphant story, full of dignity and struggle. However, at the same time it is a tragic reminder of how talent and passion could take a backseat to looks and image for black women. Effie, the brown-skinned, full-figured woman, is consistently put in the shadows behind Deena, the slender, fair-skinned woman with "good" hair, who gets branded as the face and voice of the group even though Effie is far the better singer.

In America today we have a bunch of beautiful, big-breasted, full-figured Mo'Niques, Queen Latifahs, and Jennifer Hudsons and countless others in the African-American community. We also have black women like Oprah Winfrey, who has been public about the pain and trauma she experienced surrounding weight issues. The dream that most girls have, especially black girls, is to be beautiful and wanted by all. It is also the dream of adult women not to be held to standards that may deny them opportunities to be in long-term relationships because they're not considered beautiful.

There are some important general lessons to be learned from Stanley and Keith and the legion of other brothers who travel overseas and come back with a different physical standard by which to judge black women. It is disingenuous for men to point out the potential health consequences of black women's weight but then not be attentive to the mental health issues that may be the cause of their weight—and that men themselves have contributed to. Studies show that black women's weight issues are related to physical as well as mental health issues such as depression, anxiety, all types and forms of trauma, and racial discrimination.

The second lesson is that there is a difference between black men who have married women and who have seen them struggle with weight issues, and those who have not. It is one thing for men to exempt themselves from the opportunity to participate in women's lives, for fear of what they may not want to deal with in the future. It is quite another for men like Stanley, whose wife gained weight partly due to bringing his children into this world, then to decide that he has a different standard of attraction.

Neither man is living up to his potential. Not only is it hypocritical to expect women to stay the same size five or ten years after marriage or after children; it is evil. Until men take a fraction of child care responsibilities from women, then there can be no fair comparison about what women can do after how many years. Studies continue to show that women have a "second shift" added to their jobs when it comes to child care duties. And we all know that stress is a great contributor to weight gain.

The third lesson is that choosing Brazilian women under the notion that because they are African they are more real follows the same script put forth by white society. In fact, it sounds much like the same old formula: if you're white, you're all right . . .

Brazilian women are slender, fair-skinned, and beautiful. Black women are fat, black, and ugly. It's an image that black men are perpetuating and contributing to.

The fourth thing black men are doing by invoking the Halle Berry–J-Lo body standard is masking their own sexuality and issues with domination and performance anxiety. And they are projecting all that onto black women.

In addition to these general points, there are some specific lessons for professional men. Blaming inner-city poor black men, or hip-hop, or Sir Mix-a-Lot for the size of black women is convenient. It's easier for professional black men, the leaders of the community, to do that than to take responsibility for what happens in the black community.

From Tyler Perry's Madea to Eddie Murphy's many fat black characters including Rasputia in *Norbit*, to Martin Lawrence's character in *Big Momma's House*. Too often black *men* make money off the image and size of black women. It has become a cottage industry. But would it be as funny if real black women were playing those roles? It is only funny when men play dress-up and it's a parody, right?

Black men in drag is nothing short of a minstrel tradition that makes fun of black women, similar to the way that white men dressed up in blackface to poke fun at blacks. It was also a way for white men to project their sexual fears and anxieties onto black men. In a similar fashion, talented black male artists are making light of, and projecting their fears onto, black women. As with their white counterparts, there is definitely something underlying this. At a minimum, heterosexual black men who dress up in drag seem to be saying that since they are judged by their size (penis size), then they are going to judge women by *their* size.

At the very worst they seem to be saying that no matter how talented they are, the only way they can make real money is by reproducing images of black mothers that are a mockery. In either case, today black women's size is the brunt of everyone's jokes. White radio stations routinely run contests aimed at the "ghetto booties." White girls can call in and laugh at "junk in the trunk." So while blacks get upset about white men calling their women "nappy-headed ho's," they are doing far worse to destroy the image of the black woman.

Finally, for husbands and significant others, please acknowledge that no black woman is born big. She grows big over time. It would be simple to say that men should just love big women. It is more important to talk about how to love black women as they get bigger. The idea is to connect their inevitable growth with men's capacity to grow in understanding the issues that black women face. To love women as they grow is to be in tune with the struggles that they go through as they have children, as they get jobs that require more time and less time for self-care, as they get sick, and so on.

Any man who has loved a black woman, if he is honest with himself, knows that weight and hair are issues that black women have to deal with on a daily basis. No matter how successful a woman is, her weight will still be used as a benchmark of her value and worth. So size does matter because, if nothing else, it matters to women. And it definitely matters to men. Men get to minimize the importance that women place on attempting to look good. Men act as if it's money wasted when women buy beauty products, or time wasted when they take too long in front of the mirror. At the same time, men judge women exactly by how they look.

If a man is paying attention, he can see for himself how those weight-and-looks issues are passed down to his daughter, from having to deal with braids and beads, to extensions, and eventually the straightening comb—even if she's only four years old. You begin to see how these struggles are passed down, and you imagine how your little girl will be judged by her hair, her complexion, and her body size as she gets older. You wonder if she will run into a professional like the architect of the Harlem Club, who reported, "I didn't marry my wife because she was a kind, sensitive woman. I married her because she is a complete package. I married her because she takes her butt to the gym, and she keeps it tight for me. I want it all, and I got it all. There are men who want the same."

And you pray to God that he's wrong.

Chapter Eight

"She Knows How to Love Me": The Secret of the Brazilian Attraction

Black men are lost. They are lacking something. Maybe it's the way their mothers treated them or loved them. I don't know what it is or how we got here, or when it all happened, but black men aren't feeling black women.

Brazilian women are more responsive to us, in a true state, than our own black women here. They are more nurturing; they are more caring towards us. [Brazilian women] love us like black women loved us in the sixties and the early seventies. Black people were more in love with each other then—male to female. Being in Brazil is like stepping back in time.

I believe that is the greatest feeling men have about Rio de Janeiro outside of the sex. Words cannot explain how wonderful that is. I felt more like a man being in Rio, and I knew the difference coming back to America. [In America] we equate things with things that are financial. In order to be happy you have to have this, you have to have a position, you have to have a lot of money. In Brazil they view good health as being successful. They look at things like being happy as opposed to having money. Most people don't have automobiles there, so it doesn't matter what you drive.

Being there was the closest feeling I have ever had of being inside of love—that feeling of being safe, secure, in your village, with your people and everything was happy. Your mind wasn't fixed on negativity. I have lived all over this country; none of this stuff here is like that. In Brazil it is a totally different culture.

And the women . . . it's not the relationship because, obviously, it wasn't a relationship. But the time I spent with the women there was indescribable. Did you ever see that movie that Denzel Washington was in called Mississippi Masala? *Do you remember the part when his aunt took that woman into their kitchen and was talking to her? Now, I want you to look at that. I want you to look at that scene and because, to me, that was one of the things that black women used to do for other women that never happens anymore. His aunt told that girl, "You know, my nephew's a special man. And he has worked very hard and we're very proud of him. You know, sometimes, though, no matter what a man does and works hard towards, something always goes wrong." And then she looks at this girl and tells her, "That's the time when you're supposed to do what you need to do. Do you understand what I'm telling you?" She was telling that girl that no matter what, she would have to be there for her man—and do whatever she needed to do to make things right for him.*

What I learned from women in Brazil was (a) how to relax; (b) how to enjoy myself when I'm supposed to be enjoying myself; and (c) how a woman is supposed to respond to a man. I had forgotten how a woman is supposed to respond. On my first day, we landed, went to the hotel. Within two hours I had changed my clothes and was down on the beach. I was on the beach with a towel over my face, just relaxing when a young lady came over, sat on my stomach, and asked me why I had my head in the sand. I mean, she didn't know me and she walked right up and started talking to me like she knew me forever. She was a woman who was comfortable enough within herself to know how she could approach me as a man. We hung out and danced all night long. There was no pressure, no drama, no problems.

—Greg, 52, marketing executive, Los Angeles

What Greg is talking about seems to be echoed by most of the men I talked to regarding their experiences in Brazil. But Greg is saying something a little deeper about the women in Brazil. He is saying that they are the way sisters in America *used* to be. What makes men love the women of Rio is that they are a throwback to a time when a black woman really stood by her man and loved him unconditionally, when a black man could depend on his woman to be there for him through thick and thin without judgment or hassle. It was a time, for Greg, in the 1960s and '70s, when a woman not only knew how to treat a man, but she schooled the next generation on what to do.

He believes that's all gone now in America. But it is alive and well in Brazil, and that's why Rio feels like "home."

While there are some tricks that the women in Brazil have, the main draw for men is not the sex, contrary to popular belief, but how these women make these men feel on the inside. And sisters, according to the men I interviewed, just can't compete with that.

Greg and men like him believe that black women have lost touch—lost their connection—to men.

Greg is a six-figure, upper-middle-class black professional working in the fast-paced world of marketing in Los Angeles, yet he refers to the old Southern values and a movie like *Mississippi Masala* as his example of black nirvana. This might be surprising, but it just shows how men like Greg have moved further away from black women since traveling to Brazil. Greg is a part of a group of black professional men who have been traveling to Brazil for more than a decade.

In fact, the deep emotional bond he has about Brazil erupted several times during our conversation. The conversation often centered on whether the experiences that he and other black men had were simply the result of paying for sex, or what is commonly referred to as "play for pay." His immediate response was this:

> *Black women need to get that fucking bullshit out of their head about us paying for it, because there's absolutely not a black woman in the world that I didn't have to pay for it in some shape, form, or fashion. Believe me, as I'm sitting here and telling you right now, you will not have sex or encounter sex*

with a black woman without some money changing hands.
And that's the honest truth. I don't care if she's your wife, your
girlfriend, or whatever. Money is going to change hands. So
when you're standing there and calling it a fantasy based on
some money, I have never met a black woman who doesn't
consider economics in a situation before anything jumps off. It
is about the money!

That said, I believe that I could have a black woman [in
America] do everything that a Brazilian woman would do,
but her attitude would be entirely different. And as a result,
it would be a whole lot less enjoyable for me. So even though
black women point fingers at the women in Brazil and say
horrible things about them, they do the same thing—just not
as well. I'd rather deal with a woman where I know exactly
what I'm getting.

While his emotions oscillated between extreme admiration and appreciation for Brazil, and a bitter resentment and anger toward those who would criticize it, Greg was not the only man or the most emphatic and heartfelt in his expressions about the impact of Brazil and its women in his life. Phillip actually mentioned that he cried when he returned from his first trip. I assumed that he was just being dramatic, so I asked him if he was being figurative and he said, "No, I'm serious. I actually physically shed tears. I wasn't bawling, but yes, I did cry. In hindsight, obviously it had to be a mixture of things, but I would say it had more to do with what was going on in my life at the time."

For some black men, the women of Rio provide a type of black love that they never had, while for others it is love they thought they had lost forever. For Greg, from the day he arrived at the beach and was initiated into Brazilian culture and Brazilian women, he was reminded of a time when black folks used to love each other—a perspective that has only grown over the years as he has traveled back and forth to Rio. For Tom, a forty-three-year-old retail store manager from Birmingham, it was more like love at first sight. Here is how he described his first trip:

> The way I heard about it was through a couple of friends, and they told me about the weather and about the women and how beautiful and different things were there. Coming from an impoverished background where people didn't do much and not much was expected of me, I wanted to beat the odds and get out of the country, which is not something that black men tend to do. For me, going to Rio was about seeing what this Utopia was all about.
>
> The first time I landed, it was almost like home, for me a place. When I stepped out of the airport, it just felt like a place that I was going to love—from the weather to the way the wind felt on my skin. I felt instant ties. Even the poor areas that we drove through, I got this sentimental feeling about it. I could relate to those people automatically. I was one of them.

There are some obvious issues with both these pathways to black love. First, Greg's mind harked back to a time when there was no gender confusion about the roles of black men and black women—a time when black women loved black men, a time when black women were committed to black men. According to another man,

I don't like to generalize, but I'm going to now since we're talking about Brazil. Brazilian women are a lot more feminine than a lot of these black professional women. It's just how it is. They're more feminine. In Brazil and like most Latin American countries, the woman will be there for the man. It's kind of like the way it used to be in the old days, you know what I'm saying? Here in the United States, a woman used to cook dinner for her husband and take care of the kids and the household—even if she worked. Case in point: I had a girl- friend from Panama, and her mom worked. Her dad worked, too. But her mom would come home and still cook. Her mom would still come home and cook every night. I would be like, "Wow!"

While it's true that the black family was more intact in the past than it is today, it is also true that the 1960s and '70s were important times in black life, when public affirmation of love for black people was unprecedented. The black love Greg spoke of was inspired by a profound respect and pride that men and women had for one another because of the struggles and burdens they had to bear. More important, that love and mutual respect men and women had for each other extended back to the Southern heritage he referred to precisely because of the roles that men played in the household. Black men, faced with unprecedented assaults against their dignity and humanity, showed unfathomable commitment to women, children, and community. That is sorely lacking today.

But not to be guilty of the same "nostalgia" and romanti- cizing of the past, it is important to acknowledge that black women were the first to show that the "Southern heritage" and those traditional roles were not without their problems. Alice Walker's *The Color Purple* has never been a favorite for black men, but it showed how the Southern heritage also included abuse and victimization of women. Similarly, Michelle Wallace's *Black Macho and the Myth of the Superwoman* showed that the 1960s and '70s also were not totally perfect times between black men and women. Appeals to a future based on a simplistic past are a mistake either way.

Here is a fact: it has been the black woman's role in the family that has been the most consistent over time. Either as mothers, aunts, grandmothers, or a host of other "women-folk," the black woman continues to raise and nurture children. She hasn't changed. And for these black men to blame the black woman for any changes in roles and love means that they really need to look in the mirror at themselves. But they remain blind to some of the real problems.

Tom's path to love is equally problematic. In fact, the "instant ties" he referred to when landing in Brazil were not really instant at all. Like other men who travel to Brazil, he had been primed by the things his friends at work told him about the women, the weather, and everything else well before he landed. Consequently, he had an image of a utopia in his mind before he left. However, the impact of Rio on Tom's life is important for another reason. Unlike Greg, who is in the upper middle class earning more than six figures, Tom is more of a lower-middle-class black professional. He is not considered affluent because he does not earn above sixty thousand dollars a year. He is in the thirty thousand to fifty thousand range.

Considering how regularly he goes to Rio—at least once a year (and sometimes more) for the past seven years—and given his other obligations as a father of two, I asked him why he continues to make the trip. His response highlighted not only the importance of Rio but also the willingness of some people to sacrifice everything to stay connected to it:

> For me, it is something that I want to have in my life. And like anything else you want, you work for it. Oftentimes I equate it to young brothers who invest in material items, like cars and jewelry, and it makes them happy. From my background and an understanding that being materialistic isn't good, I prefer to invest in my happiness.
>
> You invest in things that are internal, and things that people can't take from you. And for me that trip becomes my instant access to the tomb—to all the gold and all the riches.

He went on to say in an equally revealing interview that even his quality of life in the states is improved as a result of his trips to Brazil:

> I go there and I live in an apartment. I don't have cable or any of the amenities. But I have the basics and all that I need, and everything is beautiful. It helps me understand more what I have here, what I have to do here and what my purpose is here. When I come back [to the States], I have more than in Rio, but I don't have the culture. I don't have the beaches; my economic situation doesn't extend as far as it does there. So in a sense, when I'm [in Brazil], I am somebody else.

The idea of being a different person or having a supplemental identity is crucial to understanding why so many black men end up developing deep ties with Brazil and its women. For them, it reflects a type of connection and recognition they feel that they can't get in America from black women. So whether it is paying for pussy or paying for a place, the point is that they feel they can't get either here.

Brazil: Black Mecca or Black Womb?

We constantly hear that it takes a village to raise a child. But what if the *village* is the problem? That is essentially the message communicated by black men who travel to Brazil. In the most romanticized version, Brazil is a great black Mecca that encompasses African people, heritage, and the past. It is an image that is not created entirely in the minds and imaginations of black men. You can read "Brazil's African Heart" in a beautiful spread in *American Legacy* magazine, or you can read about the "Dance of Life to Honor Death" in the *New York Times,* and you can certainly read about it in the number of African-American travel agencies that are aimed at connecting the African-Americans' hearts and minds to foreign travel destinations where African-American culture and history thrive.

What you will hear about Brazil is that it is the largest concentration of people of African descent in the Western Hemisphere. People are quick to point out the five hundred years of African religious and cultural practices like candomblé, capoeira, and samba. Brazil is reportedly the last country to stop the African slave trade—it started earlier and lasted longer, and therefore the African culture had a far greater impact on that country than on any other outside the continent itself. Parts of Brazil were so black that the government started a "whitening" process, limiting the number of babies blacks could have. In addition, you will hear about the spirit and beauty of cities like Rio, with its statue of Christ and Sugarloaf Mountain. More important, you will hear about the regard for African people in the history and identity of black people in Brazilian life and society. This is how Phillip described one of his experiences:

> *The statue of Christ. It is so beautiful. I can't even tell you how big it is. And this was built by hand. How did they get it up there? When you take the train up the mountain, or the cable cars, and you're looking at the Atlantic Ocean from the tallest point, wondering, how did they do this? And you realize that black people did that!*

Based on this portrait, it is clear that no black neighborhood, city, or suburb in America can compete with the physical and nonphysical aspects of Rio. Even middle-class black neighborhoods can't measure up. Research continues to show that black middle-class neighborhoods suffer from high rates of residential segregation and are consistently exposed to more crime and that black middle-class neighborhoods or suburbs lack levels of "public services, school quality, safety, and environmental quality" compared with other suburbs. One study by the Lewis Mumford Center found that on average, affluent blacks suffered a neighborhood gap of nearly sixteen thousand dollars, and in some instances as much as thirty-three thousand dollars, compared with whites. What this means is that although one-third of all blacks currently live in suburbs, no matter how much African-Americans struggle to earn the opportunity to live in suburbs like Plainfield, New Jersey; Shaker Heights, Ohio; Prince Georges County, Maryland; or areas around Miami, Atlanta, St. Louis, Fort Lauderdale, Chicago, or Washington, D.C., there are very few middle-class and affluent neighborhoods that provide African-Americans with the quality of life that they deserve.

So what does Brazil hold for these men? Promise and hope of actually living the way they feel they ought to.

This is one of the main reasons why you can read the "threads" on the message boards, where people constantly reminisce about life in Rio and doing such things as walking on the beaches of Ipanema or Copacabana, eating fish, shopping in the open markets, enjoying the beach culture, the casual conversations with strangers, the cobblestones. In essence, they are reminiscing about the type of amenities of a community that don't include a Starbucks or a Whole Foods Market. It is a way of life that is much slower and stress-free than in America. It's also presumably why so many black men talk of learning how to relax and they see a lifestyle that is much more stress-free, which contributes to their loving the country and its women even more. It is also why many entertain the idea of retiring to Brazil. According to Tom,

*Those experiences—right down to the cars they drive and the
way people get around to the stores they run—it's a whole different thing. You come back [to America] and see how people
are treating each other and what's going on, and I continue to
play that role here and it makes it easier for me. I am relatively
young [forty], but that is the life I would like to have when I
retire. I can see that.*

It is not as if men like Tom or Greg were oblivious of the
class and racial issues in Brazil. In fact, they will quickly point
out when questioned about these things, as Tom did, that
"African people play a significant part of every aspect in Brazilian life, although they don't recognize it as race—it's more
of a class issue. And it trickles down to color tones—not so
much of a black-white thing. But your shade establishes your
status." From their perspective, whatever the racial and class
issues there are in Brazil, it's still better than the race and class
problems in America.

While the race issue and being "treated like a full man" in
Brazilian society is certainly a factor, for most men it is still
about the women. That is what Greg found so compelling
about his experience. It was the way that this culture influences women and how they interacted with him as a man that
was so important. It is a culture where women knew how to
be women. This is how David explained the difference:

*There are cultures in the world where people realize that you
are not guaranteed tomorrow. Overseas you run into ladies
who like you and you don't waste time with all of the shit you*

have to deal with in America with black women. All protocol is off, because I dig you. And what I mean by protocols is in America we have to talk for a while, then we have to get to know you, then I won't or can't call you after the first date, and maybe we will go to bed after six months; then there is this time schedule thing, where you can't make advances, so that she doesn't feel like a fucking slut. You go to the overseas culture and it's like, everything I want I can have today. Brothers are amazed. And these aren't no damn hookers, either! This is a cultural phenomenon that you meet when you get outside the United States and meet different women.

Black women can't compete with Brazilian women, because of their culture. In addition to Brazil's being this black Mecca, it is also this black womb that nurtures and protects black manhood. Implicit in this notion of American culture and how it affects black women is the suggestion, mentioned by Greg, that black women have lost their culture. What these men find themselves saying and believing is that black women epitomize American values. In contrast to Brazilian women, who taught him how to relax and enjoy life, and what the proper things are to focus on in life, black women are more stressful and materialistic. The obvious contradiction with this belief is that it is the same material privilege that allows them to see how the "other" lives. This, of course, brings the entire issue of culture and women into focus.

Going Native and the Culture of Domesticity

Despite how sentimental, romantic, or nostalgic these men are for a "simpler time and place," what they really want is a gender order based on strict roles between men and women. In fact, the appeal to culture continues to be one of the most powerful defenses and justifications for why women around the world are denied certain rights. Just look at Ayaan Hirsi Ali, the author of *Infidel*. She is a Somali women who today receives regular death threats for working to end domestic violence against Muslim women. Or check out Irshad Manji, author of *The Trouble With Islam*. She calls herself a "Muslim refusenik." These two women are today at the vanguard of contemporary struggles to end honor killings, female genital mutilation, forced marriage, domestic violence, and a host of other cultural practices that are used to control women and keep rigid gender lines.

CNN reported the stoning to death of a seventeen-year-old Muslim girl in Iraq because she reportedly dishonored her culture by falling in love with a young man of a different faith. As a result, the men were permitted to pull this young girl out of her house and publicly stone her to death while crowds of men stood by either watching or taking pictures. The point is that culture can be brutal and there can be a fixation on controlling and dominating women. We don't have to look elsewhere to see the same dynamics. I look at my daughter and I can recall how *Mulan*, the movie about how a girl saved a Chinese dynasty despite being a woman, was the first movie that she fell in love with. I am reminded that African-American women have been refuseniks of sorts since day one.

Of course, black American men won't see themselves implicated in such cultural practices as honor killings. But that's the point: women in America, in particular black women, have struggled for a better way of life so that they don't have to deal with the consequences of such cultural practices. It is not a coincidence that the two Muslim women I just mentioned are here in America. What men who travel to Brazil, and those who think like them, have to question is whether their yearnings to return to cultural practices of the homeland are simply based on the roles of women and the "culture of domesticity."

This secret that these Brazilian women have, the power they seem to wield over these men, isn't a secret at all. It's good old-fashioned subservience. It's submissiveness. What these women in Rio do is play to every man's fantasy, which is to be with a woman who will *willingly* do whatever it is they want. The beef that many men have about black women in the States is that they can get them to do certain things sexually, but it's not without a fight. And many black men feel that they have to compete with black women for dominance. They are always *the man* in Brazil. Even though Brazilian women are often aggressive and forward, they know their place in the bedroom—and that place is to please the man they are with.

So what black men seem to want is a woman who will do anything in bed, who will not stress them or give them any back talk or drama. And if the women in Rio meet those needs, it's no wonder that sisters in the States are having a hard time competing.

So when these men talk about being home, it's a fantasy home they speak of, a home they always wished for and to which they now finally have the keys.

Conclusion

For the men who can't get enough of Rio and traveling abroad, the pull is tremendous. And for them, contrary to popular belief, it is not purely about the sex. For upper middle-class black professional men, it allows them to scale down their lifestyle. For lower middle-class black men, it allows them to scale up. They may come for the pussy, but they fall in love with the place—something that Tom can identify with:

Pussy is pussy. Quality of life, though, is something different. There is only so much pussy you can get. If your dick is the lawn mower, how much grass do you want to cut? I like a small patch, something I can take care of and groom. I'm not trying to cut the whole world's grass! All I want is something small that I can handle.

I love [Brazil]. I like the feeling it gives me, and it's not in the tourist spots. America is a nice place, but it is never felt like home—from a historical standpoint, from a vibe. America is far more appealing to me, but it doesn't recognize me as a black person. I feel more comfortable in Brazil, and I knew that from my first taxi ride. Since then, I have taken several trips to Brazil, and many things have changed in my life. I have grown professionally, personally, and spiritually.

Consequently, men also come back feeling as if they have learned strategies there that allow them to live better lives here in America, which increases their distance from black women.

Chapter Nine

"I'm Addicted!": Whipped Overseas

Yes, I guess you can say I'm addicted! More or less, the cat is out of the bag for me now. Maybe I would have a different perspective if I never went. But now it is ingrained in me and I can't turn back.

It does make it more difficult for me to have a healthy relationship. I don't think anybody that's married should go. Despite what I think about our situation with our fellow sisters, nothing good can come from that. I know guys who are married [and once they go], they just can't get enough. Their reference point has totally changed. They won't leave their wives, because their wives represent stability. But they have to step into that fantasy for a while. You just can't come back from that.

Even if I found someone to be with, I might be able to change, but I still don't think I could give up going to Brazil. It becomes an addiction. When you have brothers who have been down there fifteen, twenty times, and then you look at their left hand and they got that band on their left hand. I know guys who go every three months.

Can that urge dissolve? I believe it can. I believe I can find a woman in the States who can make me not want to go, who can fulfill me. But will it be a temporary patch, like methadone? Will that urge [to go to Brazil] dissolve permanently? I guess I won't know until I cross that bridge.

—Jason, 37, accountant, New York City

When it was first reported that actress Halle Berry and singer Eric Benet were separating, you can imagine the initial surprise and concern. However, when it was reported that the separation was due in part to Eric Benet's alleged addiction to sex, you could imagine what a lot of men were thinking. Sex addiction? How could having or wanting sex ever be a problem, let alone an addiction? You can imagine even further what the reaction was to his reportedly checking into a twelve-hundred-dollar-a-night rehabilitation center to be "cured" of promiscuity. For men, the idea of being addicted to sex is more like a joke than a cause for real concern.

In reality, there is such a thing as a sex addiction. And all forms of addiction come at a cost. In the case of Brazil, the cost can be literal, sending many into bankruptcy. But it's deeper than money. You can hear the echoes of the cost men pay when they talk about their experiences in Brazil.

One cost is a rupture between past and present experiences,

where things are never quite the same. Black men are left in a liminal state of being, sort of betwixt and between two different realities—one part fantasy, the other part reality. Another cost is a type of confusion that results from having their reference point change. These men attribute that to having high standards. But what they were willing to accept before Brazil, they are no longer willing to accept—from a woman's attitude to her putting on weight.

But arguably the biggest cost is the constant distraction of seeking satisfaction and not being connected to women they may meet or with whom they already have relationships in the States.

Despite the existence of professional groups and organizations dealing with sexual addiction, and a number of books, tools, and resources on the topic, there is still debate whether addiction to sex is a real addiction. Yet it appears obvious that any behavior that leads a person to needing more and more of something, and not being able to control that want to the point that it has a negative impact on relationships, would be an addiction.

When men like Jason talk about the impact of these trips on their lives, you have to wonder where this behavior is leaving them. Is it an addiction or not? Their preoccupation or compulsions may not influence their ability to function, but they are not quite whole after they have taken trips to Brazil and other countries. Are the men who travel to Brazil ruining their chance at long-term, healthy relationships with women from America—or anywhere else, for that matter?

I will return to this question in a moment, but in the

meantime you can hear men like Jason struggle to provide an answer:

> *I know what I want versus what I know I need. I know in order for me to be in a successful, healthy, long-term relationship without the concern of infidelity, I need a whole lot more than what I've found. I know I don't need to be screwing thirteen and fourteen different women. That's just a distraction. It's sort of like masturbation. It's a release valve.*

Impact: You Will Never Be the Same

To a man, the one thing they all say upon their return from Brazil is, "You will never be the same." Usually they mean that the experiences that they have in Brazil have created a change in how they view things, from relationships to women, to sexuality, to other men, and, most important, to themselves.

Individually, this change in perspective and the sense that "there is no coming back" is due to conditions overseas that simply don't exist in America and cannot be replicated. In Rio, for example, there is a sense that once you go to a place like Terma, you will never be able to participate in anything close to that anywhere else. Here is how Todd described his experience after going to Rio:

> *I can remember walking into a topless bar and asking myself, "Why am I giving you my money and being disgusted?" All you can get is a rock-hard dick. All you get are women rubbing against you. But you definitely don't get any real satisfaction.*

*You don't leave there with the feelings you get from the women
in Rio.*

Morgan, a computer programmer from Detroit, felt the
same way as Todd in Boston. He was completely changed
from his experience at Termas.

> *When I got back to America, for the first three days I didn't
> want to talk to anybody. I didn't want to watch television un-
> less it was a sporting event. And by the time I went out with
> some of my friends to a strip club, I basically told them that if
> they only knew what was going on in Brazil, what it was like
> to be there and have the experiences that I've been through,
> they would never want to go to a strip club in the States, talk-
> ing to some knucklehead, ever again.*

The type of impact that Termas has on men is similar to
the impact that Mia Pataca and Club Help have had. In Mia
Pataca and Club Help, it is being the object of desire that men
find intoxicating. Men talk about how difficult it is to go back
to the historical role of being the chaser after they have experienced being chased.

These are unique experiences. But combined, they become
a constellation of feelings and emotions that men can't replicate here in the States. This is how Tank explained it:

> *When you come back, you feel out of place. That's why guys
> are addicted to Brazil—because there is no way to get that same
> experience anywhere else. You can get sex out at some place, go*

back to your hotel and pay money, and then worry about get-
ting busted. But there are none of those issues in Brazil.

What this eventually leads to, according to Tank, is a new standard of how men come back and interact with women.

You come back and you clear your roster. That's what hap-
pened to me. Everybody knew we went down and came back
and cleared it off. Any [woman you were dealing with in the
States] who has given you some unnecessary lip, you're just not
having it. You recognize bullshit better when you get some-
thing that's not bullshit. A lot of the women that you were
dealing with ended up in reserve. It was just not worth the
time.

The change is seen most clearly in how men treat women upon their return. They clear their roster! All "bullshit," or what they consider to be bullshit, is kicked to the curb, and the women in their lives are curbside along with it. But the real change is on the inside.

For Jason, never being the same meant something very specific. It meant not knowing if his experiences overseas had either created or simply allowed for the expression of certain sexual urges and impulses that he now takes for granted. In fact, because the behavior is so ingrained in him, it is difficult for him to envision what life would be like without it.

What Jason and men like him never consider until after the fact is whether this change is a good thing, whether it can actually be the beginning of something bad. Does it create a vicious cycle so that they will never be satisfied? Is the only time that men will be happy is when they are running off to have those experiences that they can have only overseas? This is the emotional, psychological, and spiritual hole that men like Jason potentially put themselves in when they go to Brazil. As one man said, "There is no going back!"

Losing Your Mind: The Biggest Affair of All

There is a cultural assumption that having affairs is simply what men do. You've heard that men have two heads—the big one and the little one—and they are always competing for dominion. And the little head often wins.

And it's easy to imagine the pathway to adolescent sexuality with boys learning about their own sexuality in closets, or from their father's supposedly hidden stash of videos or magazines. Similarly, for men who travel overseas, it is easy to imagine that the pathways to infidelity and addiction starts off in hidden overseas places where they get both heads stroked.

Part of the problem is that, in general, it is difficult to determine what is a sexual addiction. The professionals who work in this area suggest that unlike other forms of addiction, sexual addiction is the most difficult to evaluate because it is fueled by things that are internal. So unlike alcohol or other drug addictions that rely on an external fuel, sexual addiction relies on sexual images and imaginations, or in the case of Brazil, possibly sexual memories.

One way to see if men are addicted is to see how often they go overseas physically. Another way is to see how often they go virtually. How many times are they online sending and downloading e-mail and photos from and about Brazil? Then the question becomes, when does reminiscing about the experiences become actual flight from reality? The disconnection from reality, and the confusion over what is fantasy, is one of the biggest problems facing men. Separating fantasy from reality is one part of it. According to Tank:

> *That's the fantasy part. I mean, even if you paid for some pussy here in the States and if I want two women, if I want three women, [I think] that's not going to happen. I'm not getting the multitude of women, or they're not going to always necessarily have the sexy outfits on, because they've been working all day and they've been doing X, Y, Z as well as you. You know what I'm saying?*

Separating fantasy from reality is being able to understand that some of the sexual practices that one has in Brazil can't be enacted back here in the States, which may or may not be true. But the real issue in terms of addiction is whether men want to—whether what may exist only in their mind is what they think should be enacted back at home, and what they revisit in their minds.

In another instance, part of the problem is separating reality from fantasy, because in the same way that he could acknowledge fantasy, he seems to deny reality:

> *You know, that was the initial draw. But that shit is a fantasy. It's a vacation. You do things on vacation, whether it's Brazil*

or Mexico or wherever you go, that you wouldn't normally do at home. Guys head off to Vegas for All-Star weekend, right? They got some parties out there. Ridiculous. But I'm going out here on vacation. It's vacation, so I'm going to pay. I'm going to pay for it. You do things differently, you know, when you're on vacation.

Part of what Tank is doing is creating a fantasy that Brazil is no different from other places. Yet, in the same breath, he acknowledges that Brazil is not like any other vacation—including Las Vegas. Men may fantasize about Vegas and whatever happens there staying there. But they don't fantasize that it is the one place where a black man can be treated like a man. They don't develop e-mail groups and message boards about Las Vegas. They don't leave their wives to move to Las Vegas. And they definitely don't fantasize about retiring to Las Vegas, as some men do. Here is what one man said:

I want to be cautious here because I know this may potentially get published, and I don't know if I want the sisters to know this or not. So use your discretion and try not to hurt the brothers. Here's my thing: I've been to Rio. I know what I want. I know what the goal is. But my timing is such that I cannot move to Rio right now and live there. But there will be a day when I will have the ability to do that when I retire.

When the guys in their fifties and sixties can move to Rio, they will move to Rio. They'll buy them a place there and they've got their retirement check to live off of and that's a wonderful place to live. It's a wonderful place for a black man who's single to retire. They'll go to Rio a couple of times a year up until the time that they can retire there, depending on what kind of job they've got.

Now, if they work for the state, hey, they can go a lot. You know, if they work for a regular company where they only get a couple of weeks' vacation, then they can go a couple times a year. So what does a brother do in between trips? For pussy's sake, he might hit one of these older women in the States. Because the older women ain't trying to get married.

Men only deal with women in the States as a sort of hold-over until they can get back to Brazil. They use them for a sexual release for the time being until they can get what they really want in Rio. And part of the addiction and attraction to Brazil comes from how little is really known about what goes on there. Even with all the Web sites and message boards, gossip, and discussions, the true nature of Brazil is not known until it is experienced. It is a basic point made by men who live in Brazil. According to one man:

Even with the desire for lust that men may have, that lady of the night can show them a better night than they have ever had and a better relationship than they have ever experienced. That has been lost in America. So even the guys who are coming for sex, they end up falling in love. They come down here as playboys and end up being played. So they can't resist coming back . . .

I would not agree with his idea of getting played, but I can't disagree with his point that the experiences over there leave men craving more. The issue with Brazil is that it has become one big potential for addictive behavior precisely because it strokes both heads. This is why the shift that men describe appears so complete. So to deny reality is one of the biggest mistakes men make, and it is only when they have gone over and over again, year after year, that they recognize how deep they have gotten. But by then, it's too late. In Jason's case, the impact of the experience overseas influences all aspects of his relationships—to the point where it creates an inability to recognize himself in relationships.

Conclusion: Lightning in a Bottle

If you want to know how many men are addicted to sex, just think about how many men watch pornography. The consumption of pornography is so huge that we simply take it for granted that men will have their little stash or their regular allotment of porn. But we never question whether this is normal. We don't ask how or what men would do to get access to pornography if it were not readily available.

Clearly today with the Internet, men have a lot more access and more anonymity, which comes from being able to watch if from the comfort of their home as opposed to back in the day when they had to watch it in some smoke-filled room—so much so that some refer to the "pornification" of society.

I use this example to demonstrate that you can imagine a certain population addicted to pornography fairly easily. But the important point is that most men can't imagine a world where they don't have at least some occasional access to porn.

Their experiences and access to pornography have changed their reference point.

For men who travel overseas, you can imagine that sex is not always about sex. The point is how sex is used and what it can lead to.

Let's return to the question of whether black men are ruined after they go to Brazil. Are they so transformed and transfixed from their experiences that they will never be interested in being in relationships with American black women again? In the short run, the answer appears to be no. In fact, proof of this would be the number of times I had to reschedule a conversation with a brother who gave the classic response: "I'm with my girl right now, so I can't talk."

What this means for long-term relationships with black women is less clear. Despite that most men described going to Brazil their first time while they were single, separated, or divorced, virtually all the men, whether they are in a relationship or not, said they would like to go back.

The issue for men who travel to Brazil is whether this desire is so strongly felt that it turns into an urge or an impulse, an addiction, becoming so much a part of their lives that they take these releases for granted. And like a man who is stuck in a hole and doesn't know how to dig himself out, and in his efforts to get out finds himself in even deeper, with each trip to Brazil, these men find themselves in a bigger hole.

Chapter Ten

So This Is How It Feels to Be a White Man

In Brazil, I feel like I can have anything I want—from women to men, from steak to ice cream. Anything I want, I can have. It's an internal feeling. It's orgasmic. If many African-Americans were honest with ourselves, I think we would have to say that we have no idea what it is to be treated well or what real luxury is like. We get glimpses and bits and pieces of it, but primarily only through sex does a black man get to feel like he's a king.

When he can walk into a club and pull a beautiful woman and fuck her—now you've made it. We can buy a trinket, a Mercedes, or a Lamborghini, or two, and that's how we prove to the world that we've made it. Or we can clothe ourselves in what I would deem ridiculous, trash [name brand] clothes, and we tell the world that we have made it. That's because we have no idea what it means to make it. That whole world is removed from us—the world of the Hamptons and Sag Harbor is really removed from us. Most of us can't even go, and *if we do go, we're there as a guest for someone who wants to showcase us (if we're a celebrity).*

We go and we leave. There are black people renting in the Hamptons, but there are no black people who really live there. That is truly an elite world. We aren't a part of that system. We have our own subsystem. The experience that upper-level, professional black men experience, we get glimpses of luxury; we get glimpses of what status means. We get glimpses but we don't get the real deal. The brother on the block is in a different world. He doesn't know what's going on. His success is a pair of hundred-dollar jeans and a pair of phat sneakers. So what does Brazil mean to us?

Brazil allows the black American elite the opportunity to have the feeling that white American elite have on a daily basis. We are better than the average white guy, but there are always roadblocks put up for us. The power structure in the United States and in the world—from the educational system to the government, to the workplace—is controlled by white men. When you go to Brazil, which is a black country, a black city, you feel normal, not like an outsider.

White people have that feeling all the time. It's in their DNA. They don't have any limits. A white boy can be born on a farm in Iowa and dream of being president. Our dream as black men is to be successful and be rich; but it is relative. There is no way that Bill Clinton could be president if he was black, coming from Hope, Arkansas, growing up with a single mother and a drunk dad. That just wouldn't happen. But he was white and smart and worked hard and was well liked. And then his white-skin privilege kicked in.

When you go to Brazil your reference points change as a

black man. You go to a place where every person in power is a person of color, from the bank to the barbershop, to the pilot flying your plane. The color stigma, the black skin and the cape of inferiority, is removed. You are not the bad guy anymore. You are not the black guy that people lock their doors for when you walk by. You aren't the black guy followed around the mall. You're not the only black guy in your class or in your organization. It's a relief to be in a place where your color doesn't matter. It's like removing the color cape from your bodies.

—Clayton, 40, attorney, Baltimore

The first time I heard the phrase "I know what it feels like to be white," I was surprised. But it didn't strike me as important—at first. However, the more the phrase came up in conversation, the more I was forced to consider that at a minimum it was something that black men had been talking about among themselves. What I eventually understood was that black men had never experienced the type of power—particularly over women— that they experienced in Brazil.

The image and idea of being white provided a powerful theme and metaphor for men who had this feeling. There were four ways that black men were allowed to feel like white men: (1) interacting with whites in Brazil's sex scene as equals; (2) literally being seen as white by Brazilians because wealth and money, not skin complexion, are what make a person white in Brazil; (3) power of their economic ability to purchase; (4) power of skin privilege.

Skin privilege and economic power were by far the most important, but the first two did come up. For some black men, simply being in Rio and having the opportunity to interact with white men of means gave them a sense of what "being a white man" felt like. A similar point was made by Tom in Alabama:

> *I've sat with people that own large corporations. I sat across the table from a white guy who runs a major company. We had a drink and we are talking. Hell, he and I were no different, because we were sitting at the same table, in the same place. Normally, our paths might not ever have crossed. But we were on an equal playing field.*

Consequently, the experience of interacting with white men on the same level contributed to a type of romanticizing and fantasizing about what white men have historically done. This is what Tom went on to say about his experiences:

> *I saw myself as an old conqueror or an old white man on a safari hunt. They traveled without women, and it was a man thing. They came back and shared their stories around the fire over scotch and planned for the next hunt. But you always return to your family.*

Others mentioned that their skin complexion literally allowed them to be white in Brazilian society, which made social hierarchies based on skin tone as opposed to racial ancestry. However, for the majority of men, their experiences with being white were in more practical ways. Clayton, who was already divorced twice by the age of thirty, had four children by his former wives. He tries to stay an active parent, dealing with balancing children going between three different households. Clayton is also a highly successful attorney, whose firm deals with a variety of important corporate clients (other big firms).

Clayton sees going to Rio as being more about having access to power than about getting pussy—although the two are never totally separate. He makes the point that sex is something that he and other upper-income professional men can get regularly in the States.

"We get sex in the States," he said. "We don't have to go to Brazil to fuck five to ten women. We can do that in [America]."

Going to Rio provides an opportunity for him to experience what he imagines and observes his white colleagues taking for granted on a daily basis at his job.

For upper-middle-class black professional men like Clayton, who are intimately involved in the functioning of America at the highest levels of corporate governance, they have a unique perspective of being exposed to power but not really having access to it. Despite all that we have been told about white men preferring to work with black women because they are less threatening, aside from white professional women, black professional men are closer to white men of power than black women are. In 2005 there were more black male judges, legislators, doctors, and lawyers than there were black females in those positions. In addition, a 2004 study of African-Americans on corporate boards found that of Fortune 500 companies, black men hold more than three times as many board seats as African-American women. African-American men have the opportunity to hang out not just in the "corridors of power" but also with white men in the "corridors of men."

In addition to being in the boardroom, on the golf courses, they are also in male spaces—in the locker rooms, bars, strip clubs, and cigar bars. But no matter how much they interact with white men of power, black men are still not part of the "old boys" network. In fact, recent studies show that professional black men in the private sector have the highest pay disparity compared to any other group. What this means is that black professional men have less in common financially with their white counterparts than even poor or working poor black men have with their white counterparts. Consequently, professional black men may be a part of the group, but they aren't quite insiders.

So in contrast to the "insider within" knowledge that black feminist Patricia Hill Collins argues that black women had historically because of their exposure to both white and black worlds, today's black men in corporate America possess an "outsider within" knowledge. This dual reality does two things. First, it creates a recognition of power, so that professional black men have an idea of how power works at the highest levels of business and government. Second, it creates a yearning for recognition and power that these black men feel they have earned and deserve. Professional black men begin to desire things way above what the average person would expect. Professional black men yearn for levels of recognition like what they experience in Brazil.

Thought You Knew

Upper-middle-class black men know how certain forms of power are wielded in American society. That is painfully obvious when you listen to Clayton talk about the difference between black elites and white elites:

> *It's kind of like how we don't know what ants do or what termites do behind the walls. We think we know, but we don't really know. That world of folks making five million and ten million a year—that's just some different shit. Hopping on jets, picking up the phone and getting your kids into any school you want them to go—even if your kid is an idiot—because you got money, you can put them into a special school. Our kids get into Harvard on brains, or hustle and brains. We don't know what it is like to just go and before you even fill out an application, you're in.*

When Clayton talks about the power elite in American society—the group that has access to resources and wealth that black people have little or no knowledge about—he could be referring to the group of "pentamillionaires" or the

930,000 people who constitute the top 1 percent of wealthy individuals in the United States. It's a group that quadrupled in number in the past ten years according to one recent report. Or he might have been referring to the group that the *New York Times* referred to as the "hyperrich," the top .1 percent of Americans—about 145,000 people in the United States who earn an average of $3 million. According to a *New York Times* report, "Richest Are Leaving Even the Rich Far Behind," the hyperrich leave even the rich far behind in income and wealth. More than likely, Clayton is referring to the heads of businesses, who in the year 2000 made 531 times that of the average hourly worker—a pay disparity so great that the AFL-CIO has a CEO salary watch to track pay disparity.

No matter what group of powerful elite whites he is referring to, Clayton's point is that when the average black person talks about "the man," they have no idea who "the man" really is. This is especially true of poor blacks. In comparison to upper-middle-class African-Americans, poor black people suffer from extreme social and economic isolation. One study in 2000 reported that African-Americans were three times more likely not to have an automobile and three times more likely not to have a phone. In fifteen of the largest metropolitan areas 40 percent of black poor didn't have a car, with that percentage approaching 60 percent in places like New York, Baltimore, Philadelphia, and Newark. In addition, we know that one-third to one-half of African-American males sixteen years or older in the largest fifteen cities were unemployed in 2000. In places like Chicago, Detroit, Philadelphia, Los Angeles, New Orleans, and St. Louis, only about half of black males were employed. Because of these factors, Clayton views the average brother as being very limited in what he knows:

> The average brother has a limited or shallow perspective of what power is. He has never experienced power, not real power. The average brother on the block experiences the underworld, black market power, which is infinitesimal when compared to the power of a person in corporate America or a higher-level government official. That brother from the hood tries to find power in his small dominion—the block, his neighborhood. But his castle is patrolled by the cops, and he has boundaries. He may have power over someone's life, but a powerful person has power over how someone lives.

The type of power that white elites wield that black people are denied comes from two sources, according to Clayton: white-skin privilege and economic power. One is simply the power to be treated like a normal human being, and the second is in how the power translates into economic opportunities that allow whites to achieve their potential. Clayton's point seemingly is that if former chairman of the Federal Reserve Alan Greenspan or his successor, Ben S. Bernanke, walked into the room, most people would probably not know the difference. The complexion of a white man allows him to slip in and out of situations with his status taken for granted. So if a white guy walks into a classroom, he can be anyone from the janitor to the student, to the professor, and none of those designations would be surprising. However, the real deal is that the relative status of those different stations in life does matter.

The truth is that those who are in the know will notice if Alan Greenspan walks into the room. His money power will set him apart. He will be treated well. But he was already treated well because of his white skin. He would be surprised if he wasn't. For Alan Greenspan and others like him, getting the red-carpet treatment is normal.

Only a people that has been targeted and stigmatized because of race and ethnicity can appreciate the idea of being treated as a *normal* human being. Therefore, it's no surprise that other men, including Isaac, a business services and sales rep, talk about the power and freedom they experience overseas, and they talk about it in relation to their blackness.

> *To be black in other countries is an experience all by itself. I was so awestruck by the fact that I went some place and I didn't feel like I had the nigger label on my back. I went somewhere and I was treated like a human. I was respected. Among my professional friends, we call it our "local celebrity status." You walk around and people want to talk to you. You're treated like you're almost a star. Like a star athlete. They want to talk, and see how you're doing . . .*

Clayton referred to this process as shedding one's skin. Clayton and Isaac relate their experiences overseas to allowing professional black men to be normal. However, Isaac talks about an additional aspect of skin privilege, which was the sense of being in the majority and having white people be treated like black people. The idea that the Brazilians are more favorable to blacks than to whites was a shocker for men who travel to Brazil. Isaac described that feeling as sort of the "big payback":

> *The natives will tell you that they're only robbing white guys. I would walk around with a camcorder on my neck at four in the morning by myself, and I never had a problem. I saw a white guy coming to one of the Internet cafés with his shirt bloody. I actually saw somebody get robbed, a white guy, laying on a beach with his girl. They walked right past us. It's almost like a reversal [in Rio]. In the States, the police might walk right past the white guy and go get you. In Rio, I felt safe and right at home from the jump.*

Accompanying this is a sense that race redemption, or "get-backs," in which black people and other people of color were in a position to treat whites the way that minorities had been treated, also went along with skin privilege. When it was reported in the United States that an American had been robbed and killed in Brazil after going to the country to find a bride, it was the topic of conversation. And it was also noted that the victim was white.

By far the biggest aspect related to the feelings of skin privilege was the sense that professional black men could be seen for what they had achieved, or what their accomplishments as professionals meant. It was the feeling that being overseas put them in a different context, a black context, which actually allowed their achievements to stand out. Being overseas shifted the focus from being black to being normal and then to being seen for who they were as opposed to *what* they were. This is how Keith, a self-described international business consultant, referred to it:

You feel like one of the power brokers (in Brazil). In a lot of those people's minds, you are rich. I remember a girl helped me do some negotiation on a beach with some trinkets I wanted to buy. I took her to dinner afterwards. She was eating dinner with a group of friends of mine. And there were some things we didn't want to eat, so we just didn't eat them. But the girl, she was just eating everything that she didn't like, and she was thinking we were all rich. And she made that point. It was the first time somebody actually just said it to me, "You're all rich!" We are in the majority down there—being in the majority, having money, influence, people knowing you and what you can do—it was like being a white guy.

In addition to their being recognized for their accomplishments, there was an implicit differentiation and distancing of them from other black men—a type of recognition for what they have achieved versus what others have talked about:

Until you open your mouth, you could be German or British. But once you say the first five words out of your mouth in an American accent, which everyone picks up immediately, it all actually screams "money." So when I travel, I'm considered wealthy by anybody's standards, because I'm traveling on the most stable currency in the world—the U.S. dollar.

And because I got on a plane and I'm in a foreign country, it means I had enough money to get there. All the American stereotypes (about black men) are weeded out. And now you're treated above everyone else because you are considered to be wealthy, rich, famous and/or you have access to excess cash. So you can't be a gangster; you can't be a criminal; you can't be a thug. You can't be any of those things, because you're standing in the middle of this country, walking around looking for something.

The problem with this assessment is that these men conflate and confuse being normal with being privileged. Men talk about being treated normally at the same time they talk about being treated like a star. The irony is that while the average black person may not be able to recognize power, the average upper-middle-class professional black man may not be able to recognize what being treated like a normal human being is. They are not able to recognize it after being denied it for so long. Both groups thought they knew. What it suggests is that professional black men seek far more than being treated like a normal human being. Traveling overseas, and specifically in a black context, is more about a yearning for recognition, regard, and reverence that goes way beyond anything they can expect to experience in the United States—even if they were white.

- Respect, Regard, and Reverence

We often hear about how black men want respect, and how being denied respect or, even worse, being disrespected, can lead to forms of social and emotional trauma like homicide or suicide. However, respect is only the beginning of what black men want. They not only want *respect* for who they are, but also *regard* for what they have achieved, and *reverence* for what they assume that achievement should mean in their lives.

The best indication that professional black men seek more than just respect and that they are deeply wounded by not getting it was in Clayton's description of the consequences of being racially profiled. When Clayton described how white people have no idea what it is like to be racially profiled, he was referring not only to an injury that came from being racially targeted, but also to the assumptions behind what being black meant. So while the average black person can identify with being racially discriminated against, the average black person can't identify with being racially targeted for something like driving a BMW or a Lexus based on the assumption that a black person should not have the financial resources to afford such expensive cars—which most don't.

So when men like Clayton do have those resources and are racially targeted, the injury is doubly felt. One is for being black. The second is for being black and accomplished. To add insult to injury, usually the white person doing the targeting doesn't have near the financial means of the black. So it's not just powerful white people who insult and show disregard for black professionals, but it is the average white person who participates in this racial and class bias. This is how David, who has lived all over the country, described the feeling of discrimination against his race, and how he feels that class matters more in Brazil:

I remember going to this town [in middle America], and being treated like I didn't have enough money to buy anything in any store I went into because I was black. Now, I probably make more than ninety percent of all of the people in the entire town, and I'm being treated like that.

Conversely, I'm walking around in Brazil and everybody knows that I have enough money to be there. You get treatment that you would expect to get when you're going into a place to do business. And your money actually counts a lot more than your race down there, I think. I think if you're [in Brazil], these are just some of the rewards people work hard for. It should be recognized when somebody has worked hard and has things. So not to be denied that is a big thing.

Brazil not only offers black men an opportunity to be recognized for what they have achieved; it allows them to feel revered. Reverence is different from both respect and regard because it has to do with power, the type of power that comes from homage. And how they most feel this sense of power is in the power that they exercise over Brazilian women. That power is in part based on their purchasing power—what they could actually influence with their income. Another man described it this way: "There was a flyer that we got. And we just called the number on the flyer and said, 'Hey, we want . . . ,' and you could get anything you wanted—any girl you wanted. You called and ordered. It was like ordering pizza."

As one man pointed out, it was not just about having sex with a woman who was as beautiful as a Halle Berry; it was "being able to do to Halle Berry anything and everything that you wanted to do." A large part of it was a power to control a woman's life—a power black men don't necessarily have over the lives of black women in America. One man lamented that the subservience of Brazilian women reminded him of the Eddie Murphy film *Coming To America*, where he told the woman he was to marry to stand on one leg and bark. That is really at the root of what men are looking for—more than the catering and the luxury, they like the domination.

Ralph described one of his trips to Brazil:

In the airport I saw this women who was fine, but I didn't pay much attention. She ended up on the same flight as me. It was a long flight, and I was meeting about six of my boys in Rio. During the flight, I noticed this same woman was crying.

I got off the plane and hooked up with my boys and didn't think much about her until two days later, I saw this same woman. She was just walking around and she recognized me. So I motioned for her to come over. Her English was decent, and she told me that her husband, who was a brother, had sent her back to Rio to teach her a lesson. He felt like since she came to the United States she had become too much like American women.

We hung out, and, of course, later I tagged that ass. She came around the next day, and we hung out and I tagged her again. She didn't ask for any money, and I didn't see her again for the rest of my trip. She just wanted some attention and to be treated like a lady.

As I was listening to Ralph tell me this story and what he experienced as giving a woman "attention" and treating her "like a lady," what came through for me was an unhappy woman trapped in a set of relationships with black men who were far from treating her like a lady. She was being treated more like an object. Her relationships resembled something close to a "legalized" form of passing women. I also remember thinking that the man that Ralph referred to as sending his wife back to teach her a lesson probably thought he wasn't doing anything wrong, because as one man, a recently divorced attorney, explained to me, "I didn't go all the way to Brazil to meet a feminist."

I remember thinking that this is the type of power over people's lives that must truly make these black men feel as if they were white. Exploitation and power is what they're feeling, and they equate that with what it must be like to be white. So Brazil allows black men the opportunity not only to be exposed to power but also to exercise it.

Brothers Are Scared of Revolution

One consequence of being exposed to the type of power and freedom that black men experienced in Brazil is the ability to differentiate and distance oneself from other black men who have not gone. Not only did going to Brazil allow men to be a part of an elite fraternity—black or white—it also allowed them to establish boundaries that set them apart from other men who didn't go.

In the minds of men who went to Brazil, they were a part of an elite group that were willing to do all the things necessary to make the trip happen. For some, this was characterized as "beating the odds" and doing things that people from their backgrounds, families, or neighborhoods had never done before. For others, they were just a "self-actualized" group of black men, and this behavior was reflective of all the success that they were currently enjoying. However, for the group of black men who heard about Brazil but didn't go, they were the exact opposite of "self-actualized" men who were "beating the odds." To men who traveled overseas, those men who stayed home were simply referred to as "settlers."

Settlers were black men who, for a variety of reasons, didn't go to Brazil after hearing about it. The top reasons given for why black men who heard about chose not to go were lack of follow-through; lack of initiative or drive to be able to plan a trip; lack of being properly mentored through the process yet; fear of being caught by their wives or significant others; and ignorance of what they were missing.

Whatever the reason or rationale for not going, the distinguishing characteristic for the men who had heard about Brazil but hadn't gone was that they were the type of men who simply settled. They settled for jobs they did not enjoy. They settled for women they didn't want to be with. And, in general, they settled for a lackluster life, going with the status quo. In essence, these were the brothers who were afraid of the revolution. They knew there was a promised land, yet they were unwilling to do whatever was necessary to get there. To men who traveled to Brazil, settlers were sad and, in some ways, embarrassing—not real men at all.

Here is how one man put it: "There are lots of brothers who settle. And I think they're spineless," he said. "But, you know, they got to do what they got to do. Some guys would rather have somebody than have nobody. [Some would rather] just put up with what they got, just to have somebody."

One of the main reasons why men who were considered settlers were held in such low regard had to do with how they responded when they were told about Brazil. When men would come back from Brazil and share their stories and pictures from their "safaris," the response was typical: from disbelief to denial, to wonderment. Settlers would say things like "You're lying!" or "It couldn't be!" or "Really?!" Only a few said that what these men were doing was wrong, or that they wouldn't go based on principle. Not going because they felt it was morally wrong would be a good reason. But that wasn't the response. Many were excited and completely enamored with the idea yet still didn't attempt to go. That's why they were seen as being "spineless."

In virtually all my conversations with men who didn't go, rarely did anyone say it was wrong. Instead, like the brother who works in politics in Washington, D.C., said, brothers were sowing their oats, "and as long as it was not illegal and they were having a good time," he didn't see anything wrong with it. He actually likened brothers going to Brazil to Adam Clayton Powell being boisterous with his many women. So instead of standing on some moral ground, they were perceived by men who traveled there as lame and weak for their excuses for why they couldn't or didn't go. It wasn't because of a moral or political conflict—it was just fear.

Conclusion: Twenty-first Century Black Power

Black men will never have the type of power over black women that they experience in Brazil. The only place where you can hear about black men totally running it like this is "It's Your World" on the *Tom Joyner Morning Show*, and even on that show, the fictional men don't have the power over black women that men experience in Brazil. This is not to suggest that black men don't have access to other forms of power. There are all types of power. Clayton was so clear about white privilege that he never even thought to talk about black male privilege. The power that black men currently have in our communities to set the political agenda, to maintain leadership in key areas within our communities like the church or sports, is unparalleled. In addition, the power to influence other black men and boys, the power of domestic and sexual violence, the power to influence popular culture, and the unprecedented power of financial resources, is there, whether it is exercised or not.

What Clayton vividly demonstrates is that black men are so much better at navigating race issues than they are at navigating gender issues. So bright men like Clayton can speak very articulately about racial power but not about gender power, when gender power is exactly what they have in every aspect of black society. Putting all the focus on white men undermines the actual power that black men do have.

Black men have power to influence American culture, not just black culture. Black professional men have the power to determine how they will be viewed by the rest of the world. That power doesn't rest in the hands of white men. This is probably the first time that African-Americans have the opportunity to be different. Not only do black professional men have the opportunity to be different, but they can also be the change agents that are so desperately needed in the black community. In addition, black professional men have the opportunity to define or redefine what it means to be African-American.

What they should be saying is that their power as black men is equal to if not greater than the power that white men in America are perceived to have. Their potential is much greater if they choose to handle their power differently. They can carry the entire black nation. Instead of seeking Black Power, they are seeking Black Power for men only.

The sexual politics between black men and black women during the height of the Black Power movement are reminiscent of what's happening today. Black men want to be "normal"; they want to be treated with regard, but they also want power, which is also based on power over women. In other words, they want to be "the man" in the black community.

Black men can obtain power in the lives of people they interact with. The type of power that black men can get from black women can be gained only through consent, not coercion. That true power is the type that is handed over freely. What black women are looking for are not men of power but men of integrity. Power without integrity is domination.

The question is whether black men can imagine being loved and not revered, whether they can see that the power is in being loved—having that love, respect, and reverence given freely because of how they handle themselves.

When you love someone, you give that person an intimate power over your life because you open yourself up to being hurt. Clayton was only partly right in his description of power. Power is not just controlling how someone lives their life; it is really having someone's heart and mind.

Finally, there is a difference between power and empowerment. A person can be empowered without having the type of power over others that so many men seem to crave. A single mother can be empowered by going back to school because she is ensuring a brighter future for herself and her children. A group of fathers can be empowered by organizing an afterschool program for the children in their neighborhood. A girl can be empowered by getting her voice and learning how to speak truth to power. A group of men can be empowered by organizing other men to end domestic violence against black women. There are a number of ways that men can access power that is not entirely based on the models that are shown by the wider society (white males)—a model that is about domination more than power.

So while the average or poor black person doesn't know what it is to feel the kind of power that many men who travel to Rio describe, neither does that person know what it feels like to be dominated. And that is a feeling that professional men should yearn not to have but to overcome.

Chapter Eleven

Star Gazing: Halle and J-Lo Only Need Apply

I've been divorced about five years, and I love it. I can't even see being married. I left a three-hundred-fifty-thousand-dollar house. I walked away from that. I have rental property, where I rent to a couple professional African-American women—beautiful women—who I also sleep with from time to time, and they pay me over a thousand dollars a month. Now, you tell me, where else can I do that?

So I just think I'm the man for real. I mean, I'm living it up. I'm at that point where the ladies who are in their thirties and forties are in a rut. The older they get, the harder it is for them to find a compatible date. The selection is slim. My choices, though, are growing. And I'm really eating it up. I'm taking all advantage of it. But I'm honest. I'm honest with everything I do. I tell these women from the jump that I'm dating. If you see me tomorrow, I might be with somebody else. I'm not going to lie. I like that freedom.

I have friends and we're all professionals. We all have the college degree. But I've always told them that you have to handle yourself as a rare commodity. You shouldn't shortchange yourself. You deserve the best because you can have the best. I feel I should be with only stars, so that's all I chase or I look at. I don't look at the big girls or the ones that I think are less attractive. All I look at now are stars, because I think I deserve to be with a star. And the stars are out there for my picking. That's how I look at it.

Look, I'm a great catch. I'm professional, educated, I have my own money, I'm not bad-looking. The females have a very, very poor selection, with all of the men who are felons, addicted, broke. They don't hardly have much to pick from. And it's bad, but I capitalize on it, believe me.

I will work a party for real, and I just feel in control all the time in that situation. I just feel a great comfort. And I think females pick that up, and it's not in an egotistical or mannish way. It's in a true way. I know it doesn't sound humble, but I just try to be real with it, you know what I'm saying?

—*Kevin, 45, human resources administrator, Raleigh*

Aside from the biological arguments of "my dick made me do it" or "men will be men," one of the most widely circulated ideas used to explain why black men have the types of attitudes and behaviors that they do is the sex ratio imbalance. In fact, the sex ratio imbalance argument is used to explain virtually everything from black men's lack of fidelity to their lack of commitment, to their promiscuity. When men were younger, they had to work harder to get a woman. But today they are seeing that with the lack of viable choices, they have the pick of the litter. They can pretty much do whatever they want and have whomever they want.

All you have to do is listen to Kevin or men like Marcus, who is in his late twenties and can already see a change in the dynamics between men and women, to see the shift in the balance in favor of men:

> *I think as women get older, they realize that their options are fewer and fewer.*
>
> *Men know that their biological clock is kicking in. We know they are sizing us up from the jump. I think that's why wom z are most [apt] as they get a little older to tell you exact, wl they want, because they're not trying to waste their t*
>
> *There is the shift now. I've got a lot more power because there are a few men like me and a whole lot of women like them.*

The sex ratio argument alone, however, can explain only so much. In fact, when taken to its extreme, the sex ratio argument actually hides some of the important dynamics that are happening in relationships.

The sex ratio is the number of males per one hundred females. According to a 2000 study, there were approximately ninety-five white males per hundred females in eleven of the fifteen largest metropolitan areas. In comparison, there were about eighty-five black males per hundred females. And that disparity has grown over the years. And when you factor in eligibility, the numbers are even more in favor of black men.

What this means for Kevin is that he has a lot of access to women—access that he is intimately aware of and uses to his advantage. These advantages ostensibly make him less inclined to remarry. Black women are just alone much longer after divorce compared to white women.

The problem is that the sex ratio imbalance is not enough to explain all the maladies of male behavior. If this were true, then white men, who do not have nearly the sex ratio imbalance, would have infidelity rates that would be distributed evenly among different classes of white men. However, professional white men have higher rates of infidelity than do nonprofessional white men. The same is true for affluent black men. Affluent black men have similar to higher rates of infidelity and of multiple sex partners. The point is that while the sex ratio may contribute to infidelity, it is supplemented by class differences. More important, the sex ratio imbalance is clearly not enough to explain why growing numbers of black men are traveling overseas. The obvious point would be that if black men had so many options available to them in their own community in America, then they would have no reason to travel overseas.

The issue is that the sex ratio is not just a position that men are put in. It is much more dynamic than that. The sex ratio is both an inherited and an achieved position. The inherited part is that men are given a prepackaged set of ideas about what their status will mean. Here is how Marcus explained it:

I noticed the change as I got older. And I remember an older frat brother used to tell me that once I got around thirty, the table would shift in my favor. When you're in your early twenties, you're going for these women who are in their early twenties, and you're competing with every other man out there— including the hoodlum and the belt boys, and even older men. But as you get older, there is no competition for the women in your age group.

Professional men have had to earn their way because women didn't value or validate them in their younger years. Now there is an aspect of vengeance in their newfound position. One man referred to women in the category of "now seeing what they missed" as "smelling the vapors." Now in his late forties, Ralph said, "The women who didn't give you a shot in high school, now they are looking at you saying, 'Wow, this guy is doing all the things I'm looking for.' Now she's interested. Here I was drooling over her in high school and college and she wouldn't give me the time of day. Now she wants me? Why should I treat her with respect?"

In his opinion, this is what makes guys egotistical, bitter, and pessimistic toward women, partly because they feel vindicated now. So why should they treat women any differently. The related issue is that sex ratio imbalance works differently for different men. One man who is in mid-thirties referred to it as being in the "sweet spot." Here is how he explained it:

We are in the sweet spot because we are young enough and reasonably attractive enough to go down into the twenties and certainly go up into the forties and fifties and experience women in all those age groups and still physically be able to do it.

In this regard, the sex ratio is much more of a process than it is a product. In other words, professional men just don't inherit an elite position as much as they are groomed to assume this position. And you can hear it in their attitudes. So often the sex ratio imbalance is a position that they feel that they have earned, and at times with some personal cost to themselves. Therefore, they feel entitled to it. It is also a position that men help to clarify for other men, letting them know all the benefits that will come from this newly acquired status.

The sex ratio does two fundamental things for professional black men. The first thing it does is to embolden men to interact with women in a cavalier way. This is the type of confidence and self-esteem that Marcus talked about. However, it is best exemplified when men come back from Brazil with a complete "attitude adjustment." Men who would not have been seen as confident before they left come back from Brazil with a different gait, a different pep in their step. Their confidence and self-esteem get propped up as they do for the man in one of those male-enhancement commercials. This confidence works as the ultimate disinhibitor and gives him the ability to be direct and bold in his interactions with black women.

The second thing the sex ratio imbalance does is to create an attitude and an appetite for a certain type of black woman at the expense of other black women. In essence, it creates a sex premium. What Brazil does is heighten this attitude and appetite in a way that confirms what professional men should have available to them: the most beautiful women available.

Honesty Is the Best Policy! Or Is It?

While it may sound like a contradiction in the current context of lies, secrecy, and hidden behaviors involved in relationships, honesty is not all that it's cracked up to be. The truth is that being honest doesn't require much work. It certainly doesn't require a change in behavior. At best, it simply says, "Here is my situation; here are my intentions, and based on this information, you can choose whether you want to be involved in my world or not."

At worst, honesty can be used as a tactic for control, just like any other tool. I was reminded of this when a professional man shared how he was "weaning off" one of his current girlfriends. He said, "I am telling her not to get all emotional. I will come over from time to time. We'll enjoy our time together. But I told her that I wasn't taking her out. I flipped the script. I told her not to spend any money on me, and I told her that I don't need her. The truth was, I wanted her to do what I wanted. And she did."

He was being honest. At the same time, he was being brutal in his honesty. To get this black women to amend her behavior, he was simply free to say what he felt and what he wanted. This proves one basic point: in the current context of the sex ratio imbalance, honesty doesn't require a lot. If she didn't like it, he had other options. She had to accept what he was saying and change, or he was leaving. Actually, he was leaving even if she did change.

Honesty may be appreciated, but it doesn't require that professional men be anything more, let alone accountable. Accountability suggests a change, making amends. For example, for the American society to be honest and admit to the evils of slavery is one thing. It may seem hard to do and a step in the right direction. However, making an apology or acknowledging what everyone else already knows is far from actually taking the steps to rectify the historical legacy of slavery.

Similarly, for a professional man to be "honest" about his interests and intentions in a relationship and say in effect, "Right now I have a number of options and I am not willing to settle down," isn't saying much.

We can see when honesty can work for us or against us. If you were a poor black man, you wouldn't say, "Look, I'm sorry I'm broker than my grandfather was in the 1960s"—which actually is not far from the truth, given inflation and the stall in wages. That type of brutal honesty probably wouldn't sit well with most women. However, you can imagine how saying, "Look, I currently make more than $200,000, plus I own rental property," would work a little better. The point is that honesty can be used as a tactic. So it would be probably more honest to say that you don't want to settle down right now rather than that you don't care enough about her or her struggles to give up some of the privileges you currently enjoy. This raises the question, is this honesty or contempt?

There is a profound difference between responsibility and accountability in words and actions. Responsibility says,

"Yeah, I did it!" Accountability says, "Yeah, I did it, and this is what I will do to rectify it."

The point is that for some men who talk about honesty, there is a lack of truth in their honesty, just as there is a lack of accountability when men claim to accept responsibility.

They Are Among Us: Not Desperate for Housewives

Another important dynamic that the sex ratio argument misses completely is the number of financially stable black men in our communities. We consistently hear about how well black women are doing compared to black men. And we hear how black female college students outnumber black college males two to one, and how the number of graduate and professional black males is even smaller. And with all the attention on poor black men, and the general consensus that there is a small number of employed and financially stable black men, you would not think that black men are actually doing better financially than black women.

But they are.

There are more middle-income and professional black men than women in the United States today according to census data. Despite the idea of how badly black men are doing financially, there are still more black men outearning black women. For example, there are more black men who make between $32,000 and $55,000 than there are black women. There are more black men who make between $50,000 and $60,000 and more who make between $75,000 and $100,000 per year. In fact, when you get above $100,000 per year, the sex ratio imbalance starts to get even more drastic.

Even in cities with devastating unemployment rates for black men, such as New York City, or cities with high rates of college-educated black women compared to black men, black men still fare better than black women economically. In 2005 there were as many middle-income black men (those making between $35,000 and $65,000) as middle-income black women in New York City and Atlanta. In addition, there were more affluent black men (those making above $65,000) than affluent black women in both cities.

Despite all the attention on how bad things are for black men, and how much better things are for black women, today there are more middle class and financially stable black males than black women. What does this show? First, it shows how bad it is for black professional women. The reality is that no matter how much black women do in terms of education and career, they don't get the returns that black men do in careers and income.

It is not that there are not enough employed and financially viable black men for black women; it's that more black men are using their income for other things and on "other" women. We talk so much about what black women can't find in terms of compatibility, but we rarely talk about what black men can't find in terms of compatibility.

Middle-income black men *are* available. They are simply not choosing to be with middle-income and professional black women. What this means is that there is a wide range of middle-income and affluent men who travel to Brazil. From military men to factory workers, to police officers, to men who work for the state and federal government as civil servants—they are eligible and are going to Brazil. According to James, a black man who has lived in Brazil for the past twenty years, it is more likely the middle-class and professional black man who will end up retiring to Brazil.

These men are not like the desperate housewives. If and when they get divorced, they seek to take advantage of the full spectrum of women. And what is particularly unusual for this group is their ability to pull from both professional women and so-called ghetto women. If they so choose, they can become the ultimate cake daddies in the community.

Latin Euro: Hedging Their Bets

If you go to the Web site Latin Euro—which, the last time I looked, had over twelve thousand members, all of whom post their pictures with their height, age, and hobbies—you will begin to understand the main criticism that men who travel overseas make about the sex ratio imbalance. The point is not that a number of black professional women are available; it is more a question of the quality of women who are available. Here is what Phillip said:

> *There is the same amount of sex happening in Oklahoma as in Rio de Janeiro. It's just sex. But with whom? Either you're going to have sex with a beautiful younger woman, or a big, fat middle-aged woman, or an ugly, older woman. I get play*

all day long, but it's usually from women forty-plus or fifty, and if she's not fat, she's ugly.

He went on to describe a recent situation that put this dynamic in greater context. He said that just recently a group of his boys invited him to a function where a lot of professional black women were expected to be, but that he decided not to go. When his friends came back, they chided him on how he should have gone because there were some fine women at the event. His response was indicative of this new attitude:

I didn't go, because I didn't like those odds. There would be fifty to a hundred women who looked like what? You can always find one or two dime pieces, but then I'm competing with a hundred niggas for those two. In Brazil, I like those odds. There you can break up with one and always get another that looks just as good.

The issue that he and others tend to make is that although there are more professional women than there are professional men—by occupation, at least—there is still competition for them. In addition, those who do look good act a certain way. Thomas, who spends much of his time in Rio, said:

One thing about Brazilian women is that in addition to being beautiful, they always smell good. They take like five showers a day and they wash their hair a lot—all of which is prevalent. Women in America who are beautiful have the air of a queen, looking for diamonds to be thrown at their feet. You can find that same beauty in the streets of Brazil, in any town. You can find them all over Rio. They are a dime a dozen and they don't act like you have to throw diamonds at their feet.

Brazil removes all the competition for beautiful women because they are so plentiful; men don't have to work to have access to the best-looking women. That is the sex ratio that men who travel overseas want. The way the sex ratio works is that it creates a premium not just for access but for access to the so-called best of the best, and that is what Brazil supposedly provides and helps to create an idea around.

Conclusion: Big Love or Other Options for Black Women

I was listening to the *Gayle King Show* on XM Radio one day when she had on Stephen A. Smith, a popular sports commentator. I was reminded of the most dubious aspect of the current sex ratio imbalance. Consistent with his public persona of being very open and direct with his ideas, Smith was equally candid about his ideas about his interactions with women. He talked about how open he was with women about his intentions so that women didn't have any illusions about what he was willing to do or not do. Essentially, he talked about being honest! Honesty without accountability?

There was a time when having privilege was at the core of the idea of responsibility within the black community. W. E. B. DuBois' famous notion of the "talented tenth" was probably elitist, but at its core it had values that have always been important, such as "each one teach one." Those with incredible resources have incredible responsibilities. To whom much is given, much is required. Instead of using their power to exploit, black men should be using it to build—build their community and build up their women.

Now that men can inherit a privileged status, there is really no conversation around what that should look like. Another reason why the sex ratio process is important is because it highlights how the sex premium is created. There is a sense that even in the States, there is still a lot of competition for beautiful women. What Brazil does is make men more sensitive about what is available to them. So it is not enough to have a lot of black women available; they have to be the best of the best. Brazil shows that it is not about having options, it is about the quality of those options. One result: a sort of disdain for average-looking women develops—an idea that average-looking black women don't know their place. This is a perspective that Phillip mentioned earlier.

All this raises the issue, what are the options for black women? Booty calls, friends with benefits, sharing, something new, or being content and happy with themselves?

Chapter Twelve

"Sleep with a Girl from Morris Brown. Date a Girl from Clark. Marry a Girl from Spelman."

When I got to college, my mind-set changed. My motive in high school was completely different than in college. In college your main focus are the girls. I had a three-day rule in college, and it worked for me all four years. If I met a girl, I had to have sex with her within three days. I never talked about sex leading up to it. It was all psychological. But by that third day, it never failed.

—Class of 2004

I reached a point where I realized my lifestyle was comical and ridiculous. I'm in grad school, settling down, trying to be married and find a wife, yet there are three or four girls that I like and who want to be with me. It got to the point where I told my roommate that I was done with this one girl, and I knew he liked her, so I told him to take her off my hands.

—Class of 1991

It's funny because I remember my university days very clearly. What I remember was that it wasn't a good idea to date sisters, because if you broke up with them you were demonized by all the black women on campus. You put all the other dudes on the outs, as well. So it was easier to be friends with them than date them, because no one at that time was ready for a serious relationship.

You might date a sister every once in a blue moon, but it was rare. I felt like black women didn't date black men [because brothers knew the deal], and then black women couldn't date white men, because that was just considered like a sell-out role, so the black women were really pigeonholed. Brothers could date whoever we wanted because we were young and single and at college. Today I date everyone. I don't hold one race above or below another, because I think women are just women.

—*Class of 1997*

When I decided to participate on a panel at Spelman College to talk about the phenomenon of black men traveling to Brazil, one of the first things I did was to call a friend who attended a prominent school in Atlanta. I asked him what he would have me think about, given my audience. He gave me this: "Sleep with a girl from Morris Brown. Date a girl from Clark. Marry a girl from Spelman." After I asked him to repeat it, I asked him what it meant. Essentially, he said that this phrase represented the type of socialization that young black males at his alma mater are exposed to, which sort of filters their experiences with black female students.

Based upon his comments, in Atlanta there is a hierarchy among the historically black colleges. Morris Brown is seen as the lowest on the rung. As an elite man, she's the type of woman you just have sex with. But you can't bring her home to Mama, and you don't get serious with her. Clark is the next level. You may date her and be seen around with her, but she's still not the one you're going to settle down with. She can be your girlfriend, but she can't be your wife. A Spelman woman is the pinnacle. She is the woman you take home and ultimately marry. She will be the mother of your children.

But the metaphor gets deeper in relation to everything we've been talking about in this book. For the elite, black, Atlanta college man, he has access—not just with the women of Morris Brown, Clark, and Spelman. He also has Georgia State, Georgia Tech, Agnus Scott, Paine, and a few other schools where they have access to women. For this man, the pickings are abundant. They have a wide range from which to choose.

Romel, who has traveled to Brazil on numerous occasions, shared his experiences at an elite HBCU:

> *To the professional brother I tell them that [Brazil] is just like college. Like it was in college. Now, I don't know your experience in college, but my experience in college was that I had all I wanted, whenever I wanted. I didn't care if it was somebody's*

girlfriend. You didn't care about nothing; you just went over there, and if you had the time and inclination, it happened.

And it was no big deal how many you had in college, unless you were real serious with somebody. It was pretty much every night, if you wanted. Obviously, you had to do some studying. But every night, if you wanted, you could have a different girl. Now, that's pretty much what college was to me.

Essentially, what he was saying is that for black males, college is a sort of training ground for the experiences that they may have as middle-class and professional adults. In 2001, an estimated 289,985 students were enrolled in historically black colleges and universities (HBCUs). However, black enrollment in HBCUs only constituted 1.8 percent of all enrollment. This means that the vast majority of black male students go to predominantly white colleges and universities. So while it may play out differently in an HBCU, the amount of exposure and access that the more than 603,000 black males currently enrolled in colleges and universities have applies to all college males.

In fact, for black male students who are at traditionally white colleges and universities, one of the biggest issues is not access that possibly leads to *exploitation* in terms of having so many girlfriends; rather, it is access to so many women that leads to *neglect*, because those black male students can date outside their race as well. What becomes apparent when listening to men who travel to Brazil and elsewhere overseas is that middle-class and professional black males' sexuality is forged and consolidated in colleges and universities.

Sex 101: Jacking Jill

Education is one of the basic platforms that allow black people to enter the middle class and become professionals. Unlike whites, who can rely on inheritance and assets to achieve middle-class status, black people have to go to school. For males, particularly black males, college life is also the beginning of an "informal education" about being in relationships with women, particularly black women. It therefore has a tremendous impact on their adult lives. The experiences that black males have in college, both at the undergraduate and graduate school level, are probably the most important social context for the beginning of black middle-class and professional sexuality. Here is how Dale, class of 1991, who went to a big university in the Midwest, talked about what college meant to him:

> *When I got to college, which was in contrast to my high school experience, black women started to notice me. It was just a different world and a different experience—one that I kind of longed for in high school, but I guess that women look for different things as they mature.*

For Dale, college was when he began to get noticed. He was beginning to be seen by black women. He attributed this to the natural maturation process of females and the changes in what women emphasized. In high school, it might be more about popularity, athletics, or who is the "superior-looking" guy. In college, the idea is that women begin to look for stability. What college mainly did for him was to allow relationships to unfold in ways that they did not and could not before.

"You're on campus, you know you are there for four years," Dale said. "At that stage of the game, you're living on your own, in a dorm or an apartment. You have a television and a couch, and you need a woman in there, too. I just felt like that's what people assumed was supposed to happen at that stage."

One of the things that he and other adult males talked about was the shift that the college experience made in their lives. This shift involved two fundamental things: the change in the quantity of black women, and the change in the quality of black women they had access to.

For many black males, going to college becomes their first experience with the skewed numbers that they will have to deal with for the rest of their professional lives. No matter what their individual characteristics were in high school, they become part of a class of black males who are granted status and esteem simply by being in college. As Maurice said, "Simply being a black man in college makes you a star. You don't have to be brilliant; you are brilliant by definition, by where you are. And it gives you a special place and a special position."

Black males start to deal with the reality of overexposure and overaccess to black women when they get to college. Aaron, class of 2004, a graduate of a small liberal arts college on the East Coast, observed, "The numbers thing really sets your frame of reference because you kind of intuitively know that if you work hard and study hard, then you really can take advantage of the system."

And the system includes relationships between males and females. For a lot of men, this access leads to multiple relationships, which was an issue that Aaron had.

The phrase "sowing your wild oats" definitely applies to college. It is a field of sowing. Basically you sharpen your skills and perfect your game. As a freshman, you're out all the time. But by the time you're a junior and senior, you know what works for you; you know your territory; you become more discreet.

Sowing oats is considered just part of the college experience for men. Studies report that about 56 percent of college students living away from home are sexually active, and of that number, 73 percent reported having unprotected sex. Occasionally, this social world of game playing can also go both ways. As a result, men get played, and some get hurt in the process. So college ends up being the place where males develop trust issues:

I am really trying to think of relationships on campus where both parties were faithful. I learned quickly in college that cheating was the norm. Now it takes a long time to trust a woman, a very long time. I learned in college, it doesn't matter how pretty they are or how good their grades were, each person has a personality you don't see, and a lot of (women) are conniving, and some are straightforward, and some are better at playing games. I take the time to really figure out what is being said and what is being done.

For others, issues with trust and infidelity in college set in motion the way they interact with women for years. This is what happened with Maurice, class of 1991:

I came out of college with the attitude that I didn't trust them ho's. It's probably ruined many a good relationship. For twenty years, I operated under that mind-set. So my interactions with women in college made me suspicious, and when I was faced with a situation of whether to cheat or not to cheat, I chose to cheat because it was better to do it than to have it done to me. Back in college, there were no good women.

The second shift involves a change in the type of women they are exposed to—a point further made by Maurice:

In college you meet a different type of woman than the girls in high school. You now have access to upper-crust women and a different level of intellect. All the women I dated in college were valedictorians of their high school. They were all very smart, brilliant women. And it shaped the type of woman I wanted to be with in life.

And it is with this recognition that men first have to figure out how they will respond to intelligent, sharp women. Men have to figure out what Maurice describes as the dilemma of college-educated men with college-educated women.

Sex 686: Advanced Seminar

If African-American male students are not immediately aware of how college shapes their experiences in terms of interactions with women, then that perspective starts to swing radically by the time they are in graduate school. Maurice continues:

> *In graduate school the numbers become more pronounced, and I have only been to one graduate school, but I have a bunch of friends who have a couple advanced degrees. You end up developing a complex. If a woman doesn't do everything I want, I just get another. When you get to graduate school, you are on your way to being a professional. You are in another league. You are elite. All you have to do is wait two years—you go from college student to professional student, to professional.*
>
> *For black women, you become their mantel man, their smart, black man in graduate school who is going to make a lot of money. You've done everything the world says you should do, and you have everything open to you. For sisters, it becomes bleaker. That's when they know they've just educated themselves out of a husband.*

For many black males, graduate school becomes the place where they have arrived. It is from this perspective or perch that they begin to see just how wide their options are. Not only can they float between the ghetto and college, in graduate school they can also float between undergraduate and graduate school. The range of options becomes more readily available. In addition, the status that is given to their position allows men to assume a level of elite status not even granted in undergraduate school.

Conclusion: Another Conference on Black Males

1. Bitch, you ain't shit!
2. Ho's are nocturnal; under no circumstances shall you be seen in public except under the cover of darkness.
3. "No" is not in your vocabulary; you will do whatever the fuck we tell you to.
4. You have no opinion; speak when spoken to, bitch!
5. The smartest thing to come out of your mouth is my DICK!
6. No false advertising. You shall not perpetrate as a respectable young woman, thereby fooling a man into wifin' yo' ho' ass up.
7. Your history has full public access and shall not be concealed.
8. If you have an incurable STD, you will be exiled and have "BURNT" branded on your forehead.
9. If you have a curable STD, you must be quarantined for the duration of the quarter or until the disease is cured, and only then may you be recycled back into the public.
10. Ho's will only fraternize with other ho's. Contact

with good girls is forbidden; you may spread your ho'-ness to them.

11. Ho'ism is a mental illness, and you will be treated accordingly. The only treatment is a constant supply of dick.

12. By law, when you fuck one dude, you are obligated to fuck all his friends, family, and pets.

13. You shall not develop feelings; under no circumstances can you develop an emotional attachment to one particular dick.

14. Your presence shall be felt only when scheduled for an appointment or summoned in an emergency.

15. Hungry? Why wait? Suck a dick.

16. As part of your civic ho' duties, you shall give back to your community by participating in charitable events such as the Suck-a-Dick, Save-a-Life Foundation.

17. Any activity with a person in a relationship shall be concealed and denied in order to preserve the other party's innocence.

18. Ho'ism has no gender boundaries; females are fair game.

19. After engaging in any sexual activity, pack up your belongings and go back to wherever the fuck you come from. Back to the gutter you go, ho'.

20. You shall not have any self-respect or self-esteem or expect to be treated like a normal human being.

21. Your government name is invalid. When dealing with your dick supplier, you will be assigned an appropri-

ate alias that accurately describes you or be called by one of the following standard terms: ho', slut, chicken head, skeezer, bop, cookie, whore, and so on.

22. Get your priorities straight, bitch! Dick is always your number one priority. It comes before your family, school, and work. Even your own life is secondary to the dick.

23. If you should ever find yourself pregnant, get rid of it *ASAP*—don't fuck the kid's life up, too.

24. Don't deny who you are; somebody has to be a ho'— why not you?

25. It is possible to change your ho'ish ways. You first must seek counseling and become celibate. After treatment, if you find a man, your past must be revealed to him so he may take you AT HIS OWN RISK.

26. Veteran ho's shall teach up-and-coming new ho's the proper SOPs (standard operating procedures) of ho'ism. LET THE DREAM LIVE ON . . .

—excerpt taken from the Internet

On many college campuses today (Clark, Atlanta, Howard, University of Michigan, Harvard, and others), the vast majority of the black student body is female. This is a disparity that grows even greater in graduate school. On a purely practical level, the reason why college is important to the experience that men have in Brazil and other overseas destinations is because this is the main class of men who are making these trips. It is also significant because men draw from their experiences in college to compare with their experiences overseas. Trips to Brazil become like the "good old days" in college, where middle-class and professional black males were able to "sow their oats."

College is not the first time that middle-class black males have sex. Research shows that middle-class black men start having sex later than non–middle-class blacks. College is the first time they have sex as part of a unique category of black males, so really it is the beginning of a type of schooling, or Sex 101. As a result, college is one of the first opportunities where middle-class black males deal with privilege in a structured way. College life is, therefore, seminal in the formation of middle-class masculinity and male sexuality. More often than not, it is the fundamental context where middle-class males develop their orientation toward women.

In hindsight, middle-class adult men are very clear on how formative college life was on their attitudes and perspectives about women. Some fell in love in college; some got hurt; others developed trust issues in college; while others figured out how they will relate to highly intelligent black women. Despite the significance of college in shaping the men that they become, any number of conferences, symposiums, or hearings on college campuses are held year after year that talk about "the state of black males." These focus on everything except how seminal college is in their formation of middle-class masculine and sexual identity.

Typically these conferences focus on important things

like education, employment, incarceration, racism, and so on. However, rarely if ever will these conferences deal with issues that are affecting black males while they are there. These conferences don't have seminars on hypersexuality in college, or overconsumption of pornography and its impact, or fraternity rape, or multicultural dating, or the personal and political implications of the sex ratio imbalance. In addition, they never have a breakout session on sex, emotions, or the issues that they will face in their professional lives, such as the fact that infidelity is reportedly the highest among the most prosperous class of Afro-American men, or why so many of their black college professors seem to be married to white women.

We simply don't prepare them in the one place where education matters, which is even more surprising considering that according to recent census data, the majority of black non-Hispanic male undergraduates in 2003–4 were not first-generation college students.

One result is that college campuses are ripe with issues and dynamics between black male and female students. Whether it is black female students reportedly being sexually assaulted on college campus, or black male students posting derogatory things on Facebook, like informing black male college students how to spot a "ho'" on campus, college becomes a training ground for men on how to deal with privilege.

We assume that a college education is supposed to mean certain things. However, African-Americans have historically known that this is not always a good assumption. For whites, education does not always lead to liberalism. In fact, education can lead to more sophisticated and entrenched justifications of racism. The same is true for men. Being college educated does not always lead to liberal ideas about women. It may lead to liberal sexuality among men, but not necessarily liberal *attitudes*.

Many males, black and white, can graduate with an informal education that schools them on how to take advantage of their unique status as men. Who would have thought, for example, that going to college would increase a woman's risk of being raped? Contrary to popular ideas that a rapist is the "bogeyman" or the guy hiding in the bushes, some of the most reliable data confirms that rape and other forms of forced sex occur in the suburbs and in colleges and universities.

The research on education and the role it plays in reproducing power demonstrates that some of the most sophisticated justifications come from educated groups. We have to make education relevant to the men and boys who are going through these institutions. We have to make sure that they don't come out being less concerned with women's issues. What happens for black male students is that they get inspired by African-American studies and have a lot more to say about race and class than they do about gender.

The type of isolation and marginalization that black males feel on college campuses only adds to this problem. Getting more African-American males into college is a diversity issue, a women's issue, and a democracy issue. We cannot expect to change any of the profound issues we face without more men being enrolled in colleges and universities.

However, getting them there is only part of the effort. Once they are there, we must provide the opportunities that will allow them to get a true education.

Chapter Thirteen

"I Am Going to Take My Son": Rites of Passage and Middle-Class Pilgrimages Overseas

I see this [traveling overseas] becoming so prevalent that it will become a rite of passage for black men—sort of like how the Jews treat their bar mitzvahs. I'm taking my son. Right now he's only thirteen, so he's got five more years before he takes that trip. But I'm taking him.

I want him to see how a woman can be. I don't want him to settle for something less. I want him to see how he's supposed to be treated. I want him to know what it's like to get the level of sexual gratification he deserves. I want him to have expectations when he's dealing with women from the States—have something to compare it to.

I don't want him to have an idea that this girl is his life and when she disappoints him, he's devastated. A lot of guys can't get beyond that point of having that one person. I don't want that for my son. I want him to see that women will do whatever you want and you don't have to be isolated to the idea that just one woman will do what you want. I want him to know he can have a standard. And I don't want him to think that only one woman can meet that and that that is all there is.

—Eric, 40, civil servant, Washington, D.C.

Imagine a million black men walking together arm in arm, in fellowship, and bonding on the things that make them unique as black men. Is the place Washington, D.C., or Fantasy Island? It's actually somewhere in the middle.

There is not a community of black men in America who can talk about being happy the way the men who travel to Brazil talk about being happy. Certainly, there are groups of black men who interact in collectives as fathers, ministers, educators, activists, and so on. But there is not a group or collective of black men who talk with the same sense of joy, passion, and impact from having been in the same physical and emotional place as men who have traveled to Brazil.

I already mentioned the man who cried just talking about his experience. I have talked with enough men to know that the closest thing to that experience was the Million Man March of 1994—that feeling of brotherhood, of manhood, the interaction. That day there was peace and harmony among brothers. They smiled at each other, gave each other a pound when they walked by. Not only were they connected as a group of black men on a general level, but they were also connected by the network of friends and family they went with. Many men took their sons and younger men whom they mentored—their nephews, cousins, neighbors. And those who didn't take a younger brother wish they had.

So to hear men like Eric talk about taking his son to Brazil to experience prostitutes might sound weird or even cruel at first, but not if you understand the type of oppression that men think is affecting their lives in America. And it's not just racism, but also relationships.

Brazil makes men want to share their experiences—which is something men don't normally do. Men come back and tell their friends. Some even end up telling men they don't even like about their experiences. Consequently, to think that men would go from telling their friends to telling their family members, to telling their sons about their experiences—or at a minimum wanting their sons to experience this same phenomenon—is not too far a stretch. In many ways, it is to be expected.

With Friends Like These, Who Needs Enemies?

There are three types of black men who share their Rio experiences. There are the ones who will tell a married man (or any man who will listen) about Brazil, and they are advocates, helping any man get to Brazil. The second kind are the ones who will mention it but won't press the issue. Then there are those who will never mention Rio to men who are married or in serious relationships.

The first group of men are self-appointed ambassadors to Brazil. They take it upon themselves to extol the virtues of the experiences. Some of these men are really into communicating the historical and cultural aspects of their experiences. They are better than any travel agent in terms of getting other men excited about going.

The second group aren't as aggressive. They will talk about it only if pressed. And then they will pull out the pictures, videos, and other artifacts of their story.

The third group actually takes pains not to invite men who are in relationships. These are the ones who "spare" married men or men involved in serious relationships from what they see as an experience that may jeopardize their relationships. They are like Greg. One of the first questions he asked me when we started talking about Brazil was, "Are you married?" He wanted to know before he continued telling me about his experiences.

When I told him that I was married, he said, "Then this won't apply to you. Because if you're happily married and you love your wife, this is not the place for you. Man, you don't need to go down there."

But Greg was in the minority of the men I spoke to. The vast majority were happy to tell me everything, whether I was married or not. Some were even very persistent in nudging me to go.

Chris, a lawyer from Chicago, has not gone to Brazil, nor does he plan on going, but here is what he shared about initially hearing about it:

The guy who told me about it was a business acquaintance. It just struck me as kind of odd that he was really casual about it. He was talking about it like he was talking about eating a hamburger. He kept talking about the women and what he and his boys did there. He said, "You should go. It's an experience." He couldn't stop talking about it, and this was in just a phone conversation.

I asked Chris how he felt about his friend sharing this with him and suggesting that he should go, knowing that he was married. His response was important:

Not to say that he will wish negative things on me, but, yeah, it bothered me—the morality of the situation. I guess it wasn't something he was thinking about. He could be thinking like this is good therapy for me and that he's really trying to help me. It's like when you get a divorce and your friends will say, "Let's go get a drink." And they think that it's healthy. I just think that people have different ideas.

His response was important because it demonstrated a lot about how men think of friendships with other men. When I asked him very specifically, "Can you imagine what your feelings would be if a friend of your wife slipped up to her and said, 'Girl, I just came back from Jamaica, and those be moving spleens down there . . . ,' how would you feel?"

Chris saw clearly how a friend can potentially rupture your relationship. Two things become painfully clear in light of this. For one, women don't need to fear the "other woman" as much as they need to fear a man's group of friends. For

Chris, who has been married for ten years, has two kids, and is a devout Christian, you would think that nothing could threaten his foundation. He wasn't tempted, but the threat was still there.

The second revelation was that a lot of men don't have really good friends, or they have a twisted view of what a true friend is. To make these trips to Brazil and other places often requires coordination, planning, and selective dissemination of details after returning. If your friend would allow you to cross your own personal political or moral values to go there, then what will an enemy do?

The point is, Chris knew that if he took his boy up on his offer, his friend would not object. His friend really wanted him to go—even though, in the process, Chris could possibly lose everything.

Virtually all these men who tell other men about Brazil share a belief that their invitation is an act of love for their friends or family members. They think that this experience will be something beneficial. For Eric, the main belief is that it will allow his son to see how a man should be treated. The concern for Eric is that his son will grow up not knowing that there is more out there for him. Eric even takes this a step further and suggests that this trip would be a sort of "rite of passage" into manhood for his son. The implication is that a black professional is not a man until he has had the experience of going overseas.

Conclusion: Preemptive Strikes

Men have experiences all the time at the bars, in the barbershop, and at the gym. Why does a friend want his boy to experience Brazil? Men share it as a way to bond, as a means to be in communication with other men, as a way to provide therapy for other men, as a way to validate themselves.

The idea that you can prepare younger men by exposing them to experiences that allow them not to be in a serious long-term relationship is akin to a preemptive strike. What it does is raise inhibitions against getting married and being in long-term relationships. It provides a justification and a rationale before there are even experiences to back it up. It's as if they're preparing these young men before they actually have any negative experiences with women.

It's like a man who becomes bitter and angry after a divorce and, because of that experience, interacts with women in a guarded and protected way. Using the experiences overseas as a way to teach younger men how to be in relationships and how to accept nothing less than being served is probably the greatest threat in the name of love.

For men, the issue is the invitation itself. If you're married, if you're committed to your children, if you have an addictive tendency that may allow you to fall victim to these behaviors, the question is, does your friend have your best interest in mind when he is offering you this experience?

The other thing to consider for men who are so anxious to introduce this Brazilian experience to their sons is that these boys are not theirs alone. These are women's children as well.

This initiation/rite of passage/mentorship is like taking children away from their mother.

It's a conundrum for me. For while I see the damage that these trips are doing to the black family, I have to say that there isn't another group of black men who communicate being as happy collectively as the men who travel overseas. The only thing that comes close in my imagination is the feeling generated from the Million Man March of 1994. To my knowledge, there is not a group of black men in America who can talk about an experience with as much joy as the group of men who travel to Brazil. And that's a shame.

But somehow men have to find other ways to find that euphoria without infecting their sons and destroying their families and the psyches of black women. While I get it and I understand the power they feel, they have to know that they have the power to create that happiness here in America by working with their women and changing some of their behaviors and attitudes to get their women to trust them again—so they can have all that they really need from a relationship.

Chapter Fourteen

Mantel Men: "Black Women Don't Want Us!"

When it comes to relationships, black women who tend to be successful, career orientated, who tend to have a lot of things going on, desire a man who is equal to them. But they tend to fall for the guy who is not equal to them. They fall for the guy whose car is broken down in his backyard for the last two years. These are the guys they gravitate to. They wait hand and foot for the guy who is below them.

But when they find the guy at their same level, it's different. I don't know if it's that [black women] don't want to seem less than what they are. But they change the script. When you are a successful man, you have to do this, that, and the other and make things happen. Their expectation goes way up. They look at our success as if we don't deserve to be served. Like we should do it for ourselves and we don't need her for that.

—Malcolm

One consistent thing said by men who travel to Brazil is that black women (especially professional black women) don't really want professional black men. Contrary to popular belief—and certainly contrary to what black women say—black women don't want "accomplished" black men. It's a point made explicit by one attorney I spoke with.

"Black women don't want a professional black man, they want one of those thug niggas because he ain't got no money," he said. "They can say that they want a king shit all the time, but they fall short in a relationship."

Consequently, from their perspective, it is utter and complete hypocrisy when black women express anger and frustration over men choosing to travel overseas. Having heard men discuss this issue so many times, I believe there are essentially three reasons why many professional black men question whether black women truly want them when they know for certain that Brazilian women do. Professional black men feel objectified, idealized, or de-masculinized in relationships with many black women.

Many black men believe that the only reason these days that black women ever want them is for what they have, as opposed to who they are. It's like what Kanye West said in his *Gold Digger* record: "She ain't messing with no broke nigga!"

A man doesn't have to be a millionaire rapper, movie star, or professional athlete to think that women want him simply for what he has. In fact, an average, middle-income black man, working at a desk, in his cubicle, feels the same way because he's seeing it play out. Just because he has a "good job" and a steady income, he is a catch. He becomes a Mantel Man.

In this respect, professional black men feel objectified. They see themselves no longer as individuals, but as equations or a set of circumstances—women make decisions about them, with the objective being to get a man in a good condition.

So Brazil just makes sense. These black men figure that if women are going to want them because they have money, it might as well be the "best" women. And according to these men, Brazil has the best women.

The term "Mantel Man" came up when I was talking to Malcolm about how his first marriage ended.

"[My first wife] actually called me her Mantel Man," he told me. "I was the answer to her problems financially. I was educated, good with kids, etc. I even started believing it [laughing]."

According to him, it was the collision, not the conflict, of this idea with his reality that caused friction in his marriage and was a large part of why his marriage failed and why, according to him, he has refused to remarry.

In one respect, all relationships are infused with romanticized ideas about what one thinks they will be. That's why people get married in the first place. Perhaps with the idea of "starter marriages," this is changing.

But what Malcolm was suggesting was something different. What he was suggesting was that his exwife's bitterness could be measured in direct proportion to the expectations and ideas that she had about all the things that he was supposed to represent in her life as a "black professional man."

From his perspective, the very idea of him as a professional black man created unfair and unreasonable expectations in his wife's mind. He was the "chosen one," the "anointed one," and he felt like he had to live up to an idea instead of just be who he was in reality. He was more of an idea than an actual man.

Black women don't love men. They don't really look at us. We are optical illusions. They look at what we are, where we live, what do we drive, where we work, what do we do. They don't really see who we are!

Women love situations. And if you've got a proper situation, you can get some love.

I'll tell you what's wrong with it, Jewel. You wouldn't know it by talking to me, but I have one of the most important jobs in my city. But several years back I lost my job for four years. So no matter how or what I did before then and what my accomplishments were or where I've been or what I've done and what I was capable of, it went right out the window, which was totally out of my control. But what it did was change my situation. I went from whatever my name was at a hundred thousand dollars a year, plus another hundred thousand from my rental properties. I was living pretty well. I had a boat, a mansion, and a Mercedes.

I lost all my homes and it had absolutely nothing to do with my ability to be a man. But my perception of what I was to-tally changed overnight. What I'm trying to say to you is that in the eyes of a black woman, the only power we possess is the power that we have in our pockets and at the bank. This is the key driving force to our situation. Women didn't give a damn

what I did before I was unemployed. I was just unemployed.
Broke. White professional men could be the tool man, could
be transporting cocaine, get caught, go to jail, and next week
have a national show on television. How many Negroes you
know can do that?

—Greg

What Greg and other men were suggesting was that the
anger of many black women may be fueled by having low expectations of black men, primarily based on past experiences.
At the same time, the resentment and bitterness that many
men have toward black women may be fueled by the very high
expectations women have of them. So high that it may be
unattainable.

For these men (who have opted for refuge in Brazil), their
bitterness and resentment is rooted in not being able to achieve
or maintain those high expectations and being judged in ways
that are not only unfair, but also standards that don't seem to
apply to *white* men.

This partly explains why black women are currently interested in dating white men. The idea of dating white men gives
black women access to the so-called good life. It gives them
the kind of man-control over their lives that they imagine
black men should give them but can't. This is how Malcolm
explained it:

As you can see, [black women] are starting to date white
American men. And they are distancing themselves from black
professional males, which is all about control. Of course, they

say that white men supposedly treat black women better than the black man does. Supposedly, it's because the white guys kiss the black female's butt, bottom line. So if the black female can control him, guess what, it's all good.

The bottom line here is control. They want someone who's going to be submissive to them. And brothers are like . . . well, you know how brothers are. I'm not kissing your butt. But the white guy will be like, "Okay, I'll do this for you," or "I'll do this for you." Brothers are like, "I'm not doing that!" I'm simply not doing that.

But what do black females do? She says that she's not dealing with it anymore and breaks out. She says, "Well, he doesn't have this," or "He doesn't have that." That's just an excuse. The bottom line is [she wants] control.

In Malcolm's mind, it is the idea that black women can get away with things with white men and control them. So black women are actively choosing white men over professional black men. It's not that black women *prefer* black men and passively end up with white men because they can't find a good black man.

This belief that professional black men represent certain ideas is related to the third, and arguably biggest, reason why many men who travel to Brazil feel so strongly that black women don't want them. It is their belief that they are denied aspects of their masculine and sexual identities by black women, which is what draws them to Rio and other places away from black women.

Black men feel that when black women do express interest in professional black men, even when they are not objectifying them or idealizing them, at best they are merely settling for Mr. Right Now, rather than Mr. Right. At worst, they are just taking plain old sloppy seconds.

Professional Black Men as the Second Sex

One would think that professional black men would stand atop the masculine food chain. As professionals, they are on top of the economic scale, and as black men they are on top of the physical and sexual scale, or at least that is the myth surrounding black men. When you combine these two elements, presumably you would have a powerful picture of a man who could not only "bring home the bacon" but also be able to "bring it" in bed and any other situation. In other words, he would have both a big paycheck and a big dick. What woman could possibly want anything more, right?

Surprisingly, many professional black men don't feel like they're at the top of the masculine hierarchy. In fact, many feel like they are the "second sex"—a class of black men set aside and behind other groups of black men in the community. Part of this stems from professional masculinity and specifically white-collar masculinity, which has always been in competition and, at times, in conflict with other types of masculinities.

Traditionally, this has been a struggle between blue-collar and white-collar masculinity, the typical brawn vs. brains; the idea is that a man is not a "real man" unless he was doing something with his hands. However, for contemporary black men, the struggle between white-collar and blue-collar masculinity has also been impacted profoundly by the addition of ghetto masculinity—a specific type of masculinity that has been characterized by an interest in discussing and pursuing sex, emphasis on toughness, and a concern for physical appearance.

Today, the black man in the gray flannel suit (the quintessential Mr. Tibbs), who is perceived of as "going along to get along," competes with not only the image of the "dignity of the working man" of blue-collar black men, but also the thug who "talks shit and takes none." Thus arises a competition, which is believed to exist not only in the imagination of whites but also in the imagination of black women, too. The thug image and idea is perceived to be the dominant image of physicality and sexuality in the black community and the preferred choice among black women.

To Please

The question of whether middle-class and professional black men have the capabilities to please black women sexually is the number one issue that professional black men are forced to deal with. Culturally, the belief is that inner-city or working-poor black men have more experience and therefore have more skills when it comes to having sex. As a result, middle-class and professional black men constantly have their sexual prowess compared against other black men, especially the thug. According to Malcolm:

> *They feel that the thug brother will be relentless when it comes to a sex act. He will take her against the wall and penetrate*

her and he has the stamina to do it over and over again. And he won't be nice about it. When [women] consent to sex, they want to be taken. Whereas your typical white-collar professional, she believes [he] touches her soft and gentle and kisses her all over . . .

He went on:

Females think they know how to identify a man who has a high libido. They associate risk-taking and aggression with a high libido. So they see the straight-out-of-Harvard, Ivy League guy as plastic and stiff. I asked a group of black women, What do you think about me and my sexual prowess? They said things like they would work me over. But they had no idea. Now, I date women in their forties and women who are in their twenties, and when they get me they say that I'm a great lover with surprise. I have had that said to me so many times. And it doesn't have to do with my penis size. Well, that too, but it has more to do with my skills and that my libido is way off the charts!

He was not talking just about being invisible, but rather being considered asexual—void of any sexuality. What was interesting is that in his case he had an optimistic perspective because he happened to be of the opinion that had he been known for his sexual prowess, then perhaps he would not be as successful professionally. He lamented, "Actually, it's a blessing that I don't get all the attention. If I was hitting on every woman, putting good loving on them, I would just be all into the sex. There are benefits for women not seeing me as a stud."

However, this optimism in the face of not being seen as a sexual being is not the case for everyone. And for the men who travel to Brazil, the mere fact that they are making these trips gives rise to the notion that they are indeed sexual beings. They bring both their wallets and their libidos, sort of like a prepackaged sexuality. But most important, they don't have to wonder if the women overseas want them for who they are. In their minds, these women want them exactly for who they are. Women overseas certainly don't want to be with a poor man, or a man who is not accomplished. Presumably, they could be with poor and working-poor men in Brazil. In many ways, it is an added bonus that their sexuality is never questioned and is taken for granted there as well.

To Provide

The idea of the "dignity of the working man," where a man gets an "honest day's pay for a honest day's work" (fantasy of blue collar), does not automatically capture or reflect the dynamics of professional life. In fact, black professional men are quick to point out what they perceive as the consistent indignities that they suffer to get and maintain the income and lifestyle that they have. They point out that while there is often talk about the consequences of *not* being a part of the mainstream for black men, rarely is there talk about the consequences of being a part of the mainstream. Not enough attention is given to the reality of being monitored, under constant surveillance, and the consequences of being controlled. All of which has to do with the types of jobs that they have. There is a trade-off to being a professional black man. In addition to the success, many also have to suffer the indignities that go along with that success. This is a point made by Keith:

In a lot of ways, [professional black] men are cowards or castrated. We have to change the way we speak. We have to change the way we dress. And if you do try to do what comes naturally, be yourself, you've got a fight on your hands. I think a lot of us are just tired of fighting [when we get home], because we fight all damn day, every day.

Who else has to worry about the way they dress? Who else has to change the way they speak? Well, actually, professional black women! But presumably, professional black women don't experience dressing a certain way or having to change the way they speak as an assault and insult to their womanhood. But black professional men do. That is the big difference. So while there might be a rage in the black middle class, it is experienced differently among black men and women.

Presumably, professional black women don't feel that being denied "doing what comes naturally" is a form of "castration." However, many professional black men who travel overseas deal with the tension that the same thing that gives them access to a certain income and a certain lifestyle is the same thing that denies them their masculinity. This is what Keith meant when he said that because they fight all day, these trips to Brazil are so important. What he is suggesting is that the price that he and other men pay for being professional comes at such a cost. And going to Brazil gives them back their manhood so that they don't feel castrated while they are being providers at the same time.

To Protect

Why should a professional black man in his thirties, forties, and even fifties feel that his physicality, and particularly his ability to protect his women, is an issue? You would assume this is the stuff that only young men in their teens and twenties would have to be concerned with.

Is he willing to protect her no matter what—through hell and high water? I think that this is something that a lot of women are seeking. They want someone they know will protect them emotionally, physically, and through any situation.

So the thug, by nature of the fact that he is a thug, has to be on guard twenty-four-seven. Whatever his business may be, he projects that sort of strength. I think a lot of women question whether some professional men have the heart. As one woman said:

> If I had to choose between a professional man and [a thug], as far as who would protect me if something went down and they had to actually physically fight, I might not take a chance on the professional.
>
> In a lot of places if you go out in public anything could jump off if you go to a concert, or to a club. Unfortunately, there is really no line between the haves and have-nots or the

*violent and the nonviolent. A lot of times you go to what you
think of as a nice event and some people start fighting. So I do
think that unfortunately your physical safety is a priority.*

What she was pointing to is that there may be some practical reasons why the issue of physical protection might still be an issue for the black middle class. Research continues to show hypersegregation of the black poor, and that the black middle class still lives in close proximity to black poor communities. Consequently, it is possible that if a black professional male takes his woman out to a social event, say to a Tyler Perry play, it is more than likely that he has to deal with the same elements that he did when he was growing up, unless he chooses to go to venues and events that severely limit the access to poor and working poor—like the opera.

But even embedded in this is a belief that poor and working poor men would be better at handling their business physically than middle-class or professional black men. This suggests that in addition to having questions and concerns about their sexuality, professional black men have questions raised about their physicality. For some men, losing one's physicality is a sign of getting older. But for middle-class professional men, especially white-collar men, losing their physicality, at least in the eyes of women, is also a sign of class. White-collar men aren't expected to play football or basketball. They are expected to play *fantasy* football and *fantasy* basketball and watch on the sidelines as other men's bodies are elevated and admired based on their ability to perform. Again, the athlete trumps the geek in the masculine hierarchy.

Conclusion: *Crash* and Extreme Makeovers

In the movie *Crash*, the actor Terrance Howard plays the part of a TV producer who eventually tries to regain his dignity and manhood through a suicidal confrontation with the police. The confrontation is caused in part by the indignities faced on his job, but more by an event in which he was either unable or unwilling to protect his wife, who was sexually violated in front of him while in the presence of the same white male police officer who eventually saved him.

The height of irony and hypocrisy is the moment in the film where, after he barely escapes from being killed, he turns to the character played by Ludacris and says something like, "You embarrass me, you embarrass yourself." Forget for a moment that the character was written by a white writer who reportedly based this character on a black man in his past that he assumed took a form of abuse and slights every day for years. Forget all this, and the question becomes: Is this an accurate portrayal of black men who are in white-collar professions?

Do professional black men need an "extreme makeover"? Do they need artists and intellectuals to do for them what Tupac did for *Thug Life*? Perhaps the more important question is, Is there a difference between the masculinity and sexuality of a 50 Cent vs. a Blair Underwood? One might be more explicit and direct, but is there a fundamental difference? Or is the difference more based on style as opposed to substance? Some might argue that the urban and street masculinity is more honest because it is more direct about its beliefs.

Some might say at least you know where you stand with

urban and street masculinity, because it tells you up front what they are about. Whereas professional masculinity may be subtle, sophisticated, and nuanced but essentially about the same thing.

The automatic response is to say "Of course there are differences." One is based more on exclusion, exploitation, and discrimination, whereas the other is based more on service, commitment, educational attainment, etc. We have a way of thinking about why poor and working-poor black men may grab on to ideas of masculinity that may be destructive, but what about professional black men? A brief look into professional black men's lives may offer some insight into how professional black men's identities and masculinities are formed.

One of the main differences between the average black male, white-collar professional and the black male professional athlete/entertainer is that while both may feel like they are only or mainly seen for what they have (their so-called "success objects") the average white-collar professional black man feels like he is denied aspects of masculinity and sexuality that are granted to athletes and entertainers.

So it is not just that they are not seen for "who they think they are"; more important, they feel that they are denied a sexuality, an edge of their manhood.

What is extremely important about this is that historically, it has been whites who have been seen or thought of as denying black men their manhood, economically and politically.

At the same time, it has been whites who have been the main ones to sexualize black men with images of being sexual and lascivious. However, it has rarely been thought that black women are at the source of denying the most privileged group of black men access to their manhood. This is a class of men who may come to believe that because of all the historical baggage that black women carry, they are not capable of seeing them as the men that they really are.

There are two problems with this view. First, the reason why men normally don't judge women by their economic situation is that women were historically not in a position to earn as much as men. So it is a historical sleight of hand to deny the economic privilege that even allows men to see women that way in the first place. Second, acknowledging that men view women mainly for what they look like is not the same thing as evaluating them for who they are. In fact, if women judge men for what they have achieved or what they are likely to achieve—although problematic—this may be more democratic than just judging someone based on their looks. At least men have the opportunity to change their fortunes, whereas a woman who is not physically attractive does not have the ability to change (unless she does so surgically).

Yet none of this deals with a deep shame some men feel simply by being involved in white-collar masculinity. How does a man deal with thinking that he is not his wife's first choice? How does he deal with the idea that he is less than what he should and could be? What professional black men tell me is that it doesn't matter who the person is that views them in a way that denies them who they are, both individually and as a class. It doesn't matter that it is a white person who makes assumptions about their abilities intellectually or financially and automatically assumes that they got the job because of affirmative action or assumes that they can't do certain things financially. Nor does it matter if it's a black woman who makes assumptions about their physicality or sexuality and automatically assumes that they are deficient and can't perform in bed or can't protect them in a certain way. In either case, the erasure of their masculinity is still a problem.

Chapter Fifteen

Why Black Woman Are Necessary: Black Women Respond (Ten Things Black Women Need and Want)

My eyes are full of tears because I've been divorced for close to eight years and I've been alone enough to understand what it means to be alone and to really know that if someone came into my life, that I'm going to appreciate that person and work for the relationship.

I don't think I'm an ugly woman. I'm educated. I'm sweethearted. And I can't get a date. When I do get a date, it's with a successful man. But what happens is that shortly after we start seeing each other, the games start. They say it's about commitment, but it's really about sex, which surprises me. I would think that for men in their late forties and fifties they would be beyond all of that. But they aren't.

—Mary, 45

Do professional black men realize how hurtful it is for a black woman to be looked at as a liability? Just to look at me as a black woman, a black man automatically thinks that, "Oh, she's just looking at me for what I have to offer." That is so hurtful. On top of that, they feel they have to look elsewhere for beauty and acceptance.

I can understand it because it's less stress. And I guess less stress is ideal. I can understand it, but as a black woman, it reaffirms my feeling of being at the bottom of the totem pole. Yes, the bottom.

I have two master's degrees. I'm professional. And I feel like a leftover. I feel like I'm overcompensating just to be average. And it hurts me when I'm not looked at as someone that is desirable. I'm not the ideal of a woman my own black man would want, because as a black woman I supposedly have baggage.

—Sheila, 32

When professional men come home, they bring that frustration home, too. A lot of times in the bedroom it's quick, fast, and dirty. It's not lovemaking; it's sex.

I have been in a few relationships—all with professional men. And while these men weren't abusive, they just weren't sweet. Does that make sense? The man I fell in love with, the sweet man, I really only saw at holidays or when we were on vacation, when he was away from the hostile environment. Yeah, they were corporate and bringing home the money, but they were mean.

—Kim, 41

I hear women say all the time that they just really wish that they had a man who would have their back. Now, "have their back" might take on a variety of different things. But I think that means somebody who would just love them through anything, through difficult times, through problems. It means someone who would be there.

I also hear women say a lot that they need someone who will not take their (shit). I think that's why professional women gravitate toward more street or blue-collar types, because they will not let us walk over them. I know I will walk all over somebody if given the opportunity—not necessarily on purpose, just because that's what I do. A lot of times when you're a professional black woman, you have to be extremely assertive. We have to be because we've been by ourselves. And at work, if we aren't assertive, we don't get ahead. We have to solve our own problems at work. So a lot of us are just really assertive. And it's hard to turn that off when you're with your mate.

—*Christine, 37*

n June 2006, *Newsweek* revisited a story it first headlined in 1986, titled, "Too Late for Prince Charming?" The 1986 article states that college-educated women over thirty-five have a 5 percent chance of ever getting married. The *Newsweek* story infamously reported that a 40-year-old, single woman was more likely to be killed by a terrorist than to ever marry.

However, after twenty years, *Newsweek* reported a much more optimistic situation for college-educated women. This new article reported, "the situation looks far brighter."

The question is, brighter for whom?

This book started with the rhetorical question "Are Black Women Necessary?" The unequivocal answer is yes! In every way imaginable, black women are necessary. Not only are black women necessary, they are needed, valued, and, most important, desired. However, the reason why this question needed to be raised is because entire generations of black men are coming of age never really being invited or required to talk about the reasons why black women *are* necessary.

With an unprecedented amount of privilege and resources, black men have been given access and opportunity, and like a crime waiting to happen, all they need is a motive. The experiences that black men have overseas offer a perfect storm of rationalizations and neutralizations that validate the choices men make, which continue to isolate and marginalize black women in America.

I have highlighted some of the major issues and concerns that black women have brought to my attention as I have shared with them what I think men have been telling me for the past several years. I wanted to do this despite my initial concerns that bringing women into the conversation would somehow blame or shame them simply by their having to respond to the slights and insults that have come through so many of these men's experiences.

What I learned was that I wasn't adding to their fear and paranoia about black men. Rather, I was adding to their level of awareness about issues that affect them directly. I will not romanticize this point. Many women *were* initially offended and often felt hurt and betrayed. They experienced the revelation of this phenomenon as a sort of double whammy of having just gone through having to worry about whether their man was putting their physical lives at risk by sleeping with other men and being on the "down low."

Now they have to worry about whether heterosexual black men—the majority of men in the community—are putting their emotional, psychological, and spiritual lives at risk by making trips overseas to Brazil and other places and coming back and recruiting other men to pull away from black women. For all these reasons, I felt that it was important to let black women respond.

Below are ten issues that have come out of my discussions with black women. These are at the core of what they want and what they need out of a relationship and how they see the playing field today.

1. Many issues that middle-class and professional black women deal with as adults begin in college.

I really started to recognize that in college that there was a struggle for black women who wanted to be with educated black men. And there was a cost attached to wanting that man—sacrificing their education, failing out, getting pregnant, forsaking friendships with other black women and other black men. It was very desirable for black women to be with a black man on campus.

While my desire was to be with a black man, I was not willing to go through what I saw other black women go through to get one, so I kept to myself.

Looking back, many black women can see many of the issues confronting them as adult women as beginning in college. However, because of their youth, the impact of "educating themselves out of a husband" has not set in yet. The range of options that middle-class and professional black males start to explore begins as early as college and is often solidified in graduate school.

Whether they are at a historically black college or a predominantly white university, black women have to deal with black male students' ability to "float between the ghetto and college campus." In contrast to white women, who historically went to college to get their "MRS degree," black women started the process of "educating themselves out of a husband." Black male college students have to be made aware that women often have to make a choice between a man and an education. White women can have both.

Black men need to be accountable to black women, even at an early age.

2. Middle-class and professional black women want understanding to go both ways.

We deal with discrimination; we deal with being not seen for what we can really do; we deal with the same pressures black men go through. The black man feels like he has to go through it twice as much because he's at the bottom of the totem pole.

We understand that: we really do. But I think a lot of times, black men are just so easy to write off a black woman, not understanding that the struggle is the same for us, too. They're not going through it alone. And it's a slap in our faces to go get an Asian or some other woman, because they think it's easier for them.

Many black women desperately want to understand why men do what they do, and how professional black men's experiences make them the men they are. However, middle-class and professional black women also want middle-class and professional black men to understand their situations. They want black men to know that despite all the ideas about black women being "less threatening" than black men as competitors in the workforce, that doesn't give black women a free pass. More often than not, serious, intelligent, sharp black women are rarely embraced in the workforce and often have to deal with a level of scrutiny and censorship that all serious black people have always had to deal with. This does not deny the unique struggles of black men in the workplace. But given that black men make more than black women in every economic category, it does suggest that this idea that black women serve as a "buffer" is more myth than reality.

3. Women want men to be providers, but not just in a strictly economic sense.

When you are a female who's making a decent amount of money, the things that guys are offering, which a lot of times tend to be the material things, are not the things that we're seeking. We're looking for other things. And I think a lot of men haven't been trained how to offer that.

The things that I hear black women say they're looking for is somebody they can discuss spirituality with. They are look-ing for somebody who they can discuss current events with, somebody who, when they come home from work and had a bad day, is willing to listen to them. They want somebody who can encourage them and inspire them. And I think a lot of times we're such a material society that some men feel like the only thing they have to offer is taking you out to dinner or material things like that. For a lot of women who are able to achieve those things on their own, I think we're looking for more emotional stability and not necessarily financial stabil-ity. That's always good, too. I mean, I guess, I don't want a guy who doesn't have a job but can make me laugh. That's all great, but we got bills to pay.

The idea that professional black women want black men mostly for their money is probably the most dominant idea about contemporary relationships between black men and women. Professional black men feel confident in the idea that they would never choose a woman because of her financial status. Part of the problem here is that the women that black professional men have married outside the race tended to be women of lower economic status.

So if black women are guilty of looking at men as providers, then all women are guilty of the same thing. Nothing should single out black women in this regard. The other problem with saying this is that rarely do men stop to acknowledge that it is exactly their financial position that allows them not to be concerned with a woman's financial stature. Men don't acknowledge that the premium or value that they put into choosing women is often based more on how she looks or how she behaves.

4. Black women do struggle with the issue of settling and choosing the right men.

Unfortunately, too many women, professional women, have settled. And when I say "settle," I mean with a guy who is professional, who they get along with and everything is cool, but there is no real burning fire, no passion. Women are looking at can they have a family with this man, instead of whether asking if he is my soul mate, the man I want to spend the rest of my life with.

Most research on marital quality shows that married black women have lower satisfaction scores than do women of other races.

Some of the internal battles that women struggle with are choosing the right person given the options that are available to them. This idea of choosing stability over passion is something that grows more intense as women age and is exacerbated by the sex ratio/career imbalance.

Men have a unique opportunity to help in this process. When men start to acknowledge the intense fear of loneliness and isolation that begins to settle into a woman's spirit is when men can be more responsible in their interactions with women.

It is natural and inevitable that women have criteria for the types of men they want to share their lives with, and that those criteria change over time. Professional black men don't have to be insulted or intimidated by the natural maturation process and automatically assume that black women don't want them as individuals. More important, black adult men also go through their own maturation process. The question is whether the criteria for adult black male aging or maturation include settling.

5. Black women's sexuality is as nuanced as any other women's sexuality.

I think a lot of our sexual issues go back to how we were raised. By far, white girls experience wholly different types of sex by the time they were seniors [in high school] than most black girls. I remember being in high school, and basically we felt like if you sucked a dick you were a flat-out [whore] like a hundred percent. And I think a lot of black women grow up with that kind of mentality. You don't want to be considered a whore.

As black women, we're told that white girls do that kind of stuff. We just didn't. The really freaky girls did that, and no one wanted to be like them. I think that other cultures, for whatever reason, [and I know white women in particular] are a lot more open to sexual experimentation than black women are. That being said, I'm not sure that black men are communicating their needs sexually. The time to introduce anal sex with somebody is not when you are in bed; you need to talk about it first. Don't just start poking somebody and then think they aren't down with the program because they aren't comfortable doing it at that time.

Black women are neither freaks nor prudes. Rather, their sexual repertoire is as nuanced as anyone else's. However, black women's sexuality is also deeply tied to a sense of intimacy and dignity and relationships. Black professional women are willing to do things sexually with a man when they feel comfortable giving themselves in a way that might be perceived as demeaning or defiling. The level and type of sex that a black woman is willing to have is based on how much she feels protected and valued in the relationship. It's really up to the man to get what he needs sexually from that woman—he first has to be worthy and make her feel that he's worthy to have the anal sex, the oral sex, the threesomes (okay, maybe this one is pushing it), or whatever else his fantasies are. More often than not, he can have them all with his black woman. He just has to communicate with her and make her feel comfortable.

6. Black women recognize that many middle-class and professional black men choose women who are subordinate to them.

There are professional guys that I know who might have wives, may have girlfriends, but a lot of them regularly keep a twenty-one-year-old waitress or a twenty-two-year-old stripper or somebody like that in their lives who they basically "help out financially," for lack of a better term. They are cake daddies to the less fortunate females they run into.

Middle-class and professional black men who choose subordinate women because they feel as if they have nothing to offer professional or older black women, and enjoy molding or shaping younger or less accomplished women, are, on a personal level, simply not willing to grow.

On a group and community level, they are perpetuating a type of "underdevelopment" among black people that does not allow younger men to see the potential that talented adult men and women can achieve when they are working together.

7. Black women struggle with issues of sexuality within the context of their spirituality.

A lot of women that I know are attempting to practice celibacy. Often they fall off the wagon, but they're at least trying. A lot of times once you stop having sex, your phone does not ring, period.

The men going to Brazil are looking to other women because I think that a lot of women who are professional who are my age are pretty much saying, "If we're going to have sex, [I need to know] that there is more in this for me—like marriage." And for a lot of men that's just not realistic.

Black women's issues with adult sexuality often involve the conflict of seeking a closer relationship with God. Black men's resistance to a religious life is one of the primary reasons for a disconnection between adult black men and women. Men's fear of religious growth is rooted in their fear of obedience and giving up privileges, and the fear of another man (the preacher) having power over their wives' lives.

This not only brings black women into conflict about their spiritual and physical needs; it often forces them to choose between what they think is right for their soul and what they feel is right for their physical lives. For men, the lack of a religious life becomes one of the major reasons why they focus on their external and material lives and rarely grow deeper as men. For men who travel to Brazil, they circumvent this issue by feeling "spiritually" connected to something greater than they are when in fact it requires no discipline or sacrifice on their part whatsoever.

8. Black women do desire professional masculinity.

I can value the switch. If [black men] have to act one way in front of white people but they have a sense of who they really are, I understand that. You've got to do what you've got to do to survive. But if you're selling out, that's another thing.

It's similar to what I have to go through. And I'm attracted to someone who understands me and what I've been through. That's what I would want from someone—to understand what I'm going through. I think professional black men can be the most sexy men as long as they don't lose themselves.

When black women question or challenge professional black men about their manhood, it is not about their masculinity or sexuality. What they typically want from professional black men is evidence that they can successfully negotiate the challenges of being professional without adopting the attitudes and beliefs of the environments that they work in. Women want to know that black men can leave their corporate world and still interact in environments they came from.

The belief that professional black women want or prefer thugs sexually is one of the greatest insecurities that middle-class men have. As a result, they either overcompensate and act like something they are not, or they choose to assimilate totally into white culture. If there is any truth to the idea that middle-class and professional black women want or prefer thugs, it is based on the idea that a "thug" black man will have their back and will have the heart to stand up for what he believes.

9. Black women do acknowledge the issues of giving up some of their personal power.

I have three degrees, and am working on my Ph.D.; I bought a house. I have a job. I have a wonderful family and friends. I did that all without a man. There is a part of me

that says, "Where were you when I needed you last winter?"
Where was the man to shovel my snow and help bring the
grocery bags in?

Anything that I've ever accomplished in my life, God and
my parents have helped me do it. There is no man who helped
me do anything. So part of me says, "I've come this far; why do
I need you?" But the other part of me says, "I am damn tired of
being alone." And that is the honest-to-God truth.

I think that most other women would tell you that it is so
tiresome to get up every morning and have to do all these things
on your own, to come home to your house that you bought but
there's no one there to say, "Hey, you want something to eat?"
or "How was your day?" or any of that. That is tiresome. And
I think that there's a big part of me that would like to just hand
it to somebody and just accept their assistance. That, to me, is
the biggest hurdle that I would have to surmount, and I know
that other professional women that I have dealt with who are
in the same boat as me—single, no kids, done the thing, got
it together. They seem in control of every aspect of their lives
from the outside. But it's hard sometimes.

10. Black women want the truth in all its forms.

I had an experience with somebody where we dated for
two months. He courted me for six months before we got to-
gether. Two months into the relationship, we're at dinner, and
he tells me he's getting married. Not to me.

I think that's dirty. And my comment was, "Why would
you involve yourself with me? If you knew you already have

somebody and you were thinking about marrying that person, why would you date me?"

What he was doing was stringing me along because he had other women. He wanted to keep me in the portfolio just in case. But he wasn't going to commit to anything, because he had any number of women he could choose from.

Black women have talked about sisters who have gotten ulcers worrying about if their man was out cheating on them. They have described having friends who have had nervous breakdowns over trying to find evidence of their men cheating on them. The lack of trust within relationships robs adult couples of the willingness, the civility, and the sacrifice that is necessary to be in long-term relationships. For men, this involves telling the truth! However, it also requires that their behaviors be rooted in truth.

And the truth is that men can *choose* to behave in honest, open ways if they want to.

Notes

The following notes are intended to help readers further explore some of the topics of this book. For a more extensive bibliography on subjects such as the black middle class, men's issues, and sex tourism, please refer to www.jewelwoods.com or renaissancemaleproject.com.

Preface: Are Black Women Necessary?

The idea of the "Love Jones Cohort" has recently emerged in research on the black middle class to describe men and women within the black middle class who are Single And Living Alone (SALA). According to a recent report, "The Emerging Black Middle Class: Single and Living Alone," in 1980 the marriage rate among the black middle class was 64.6%, in 1990 57.8%, and in 2000 41%. Corresponding to this dramatic decline, SALAs have emerged as the third largest category in the black community.

In calling Isaac a "good man" or "catch," I'm using vernacular terms describing "marriage-worthy black men" who are "alive, legally employed, disease-free, addiction-free, never been to jail, not crazy or abusive and actually *want* to get married." A spirited debate about the term can be found at www.blackfeminism.org. Statistics on black males with a college degree can be found in the U.S. Census Bureau's Special Report from 2000, "We The People: Blacks In The United States." For a quick reference on the change in marriage structure among African-Americans, refer to the fact sheet "Marriage and African-Americans" provided by the Joint Center For Political and economic studies (www.jointcenter.org/DB/factsheet/marital.htm). For information on the trends in inter-racial marriages during the 1990s, theories of "assertive mating" and hypogamy, refer to the article "Social Boundaries and Marital Assimilation: Interpreting Trends in Racial & Ethnic Intermarriage" in the February 2007 issue of the *American Sociological Review*.

The question of whether Black women are "necessary" is a play on Maureen Dowd's question, "Are Men Necessary?" Dowd's assertion that men prefer "subordinate" women has been critiqued by social scientists such as Stephanie Coontz, who argued in a recent *Boston Globe* article that educated women actually have a better chance of marrying than other women. Still, the idea of the marriage gap has a firm grip on the Black popular imagination, often cited in articles like "TOO MANY BRIDES, TOO FEW BROTHERS" written in the *Detroit Free Press*, or "Marriage is for White People" written in the *Washington Post*.

Introduction: Biggest Secret in Black America

As Keith Boykin argued in *Beyond The Down Low*, one of the main reasons gay and bisexual black men live "on the down low" is that they don't feel comfortable revealing themselves in a culture and a community that does not protect them. However, his book overlooked how heterosexual black men also live in a state of "down low" because they are not allowed to reveal certain things about their lives because of what some refer to as "compulsive heterosexuality" or "hegemonic masculinity."

While a few recent articles explore black men's experiences of anger, bitterness, frustration, guilt, shame, anxiety, the sad reality is that most males are not encouraged to participate in self-exploration and few ever come to the point of self-clarification. Recent estimates suggest that women go to therapy at least twice as often as men. Including informal networks of support such as the church, friends, and co-workers increases that ratio to upwards of 10-to-1.

There are conceptual approaches that can help us better understand men. The New Sociology of Masculinity (NSM), initiated in the 1980s, has produced two decades of important theoretical and empirical work on men's lives in the areas of health (Williams, 2003), education (Ferguson, 2000; Barajas & Pierce 2001; Salazar, 2001), sports (Messner, 2002; Sabo et al, 2000), crime and violence (Messerschmidt, 2000; Anderson & Umberson, 2001; Morrell, 2001), and sexual identities (Connell, 1992). Similarly, the New Psychology of Masculinity (NPM) is producing important studies in the areas of depression, intimate partner abuse, psychological distress

(Eiseler et al, 2000; Levant, 1996; Shepard, 2000). These research traditions share an interest in destabilizing gender in ways that elucidate men's lives along the axes of power, privilege, oppression, and social justice. However, we generally still tend to talk about men in quite uncritical ways.

Chapter 2: "How My Dick Spent the Summer"

Christopher Columbus and other famous "explorers" represent not only the economic and political penetration of Third World countries in terms of land, labor, and politics, but also their social and sexual penetration in terms of access to indigenous women. Joan Nagel demonstrates that gender and sexuality have always been part of men's—particularly European males'—relationships with other countries in her book, *Race, Ethnicity, and Sexuality: Intimate Intersections, Forbidden Frontiers.*

Sex tourism has been described by Franck Michel as a "mercantile form of extreme leisure with its roots in prostitution" and a "modern version of the old colonial attitudes towards the world." Traveling overseas to have experiences with Third World women has long been the purview of European males. In Cuba, for example, the majority of sexual tourists are Italian, Spanish, and Canadian. Most studies focus on the role of IMF loans, structural adjustment policies, and the move of countries to adopt tourism as a strategy for economic development, while others focus on the role of race (Seabrook, 1996; Kruhse-MountBurton, 1995; O'Connell, 1995). According to Davidson, in Cuba white men often act out racial fantasies, sometimes calling black women niggers. Similarly, many Asian cities are prime destinations of European males. Thailand's Bangkok and Pattaya are known as "Adult Disneylands." However, no study has focused on the way that black male sex tourists participate in this unique form of racialization or "othering."

A recent analysis of 2006 data obtained from MediaMark Research, the most authoritative source for travel data, revealed that Black males make up 62% of blacks that travel to South America compared to 38% of black females. In comparison, black males make up only 51% of blacks that travel to Africa compared to 49% of black females. White males make up 72% of travelers to South East Asia compared to 28% of white females. This data demonstrates the gendered nature of male travel patterns overseas.

The black men presented in this book differ drastically from other men found in the literature on sexual tourism in three fundamental ways. First, their intent seems not to be to go "Find Them, Fuck Them, & Forget Them"—so often noted in research on men who participate in sex tourism. Second, the central role of group experience among black men differs markedly from white males, who often rely on individual experiences. Third, the development of transnational identities appears to follow a different process than in White European or White North American males.

Chapter 3: "Just Drinking and Sexing"

Although hip-hop perpetuates the belief that "ghetto" black men are the most potent sexual beings around, this is not borne out by the evidence. First, men with college

degrees have more sexual partners than those with less education. Second, research demonstrates that African-American
men have sex about as often as white men, and Hispanics have
a slighter higher rate than both. In fact, black men are actually less "potent" sexually than white men in terms of certain
measures like longevity of sex, frequency, and women's reports
of sexual satisfaction: 90% of white men have sex between
15 minutes to 1 hour or more, compared to 87% of Hispanic
men, and 85% of black men. Further, there is as much sex
in the suburbs as there is in cities. An interesting body of
research has explored the relationship between sex and social
class, concluding that since the 1940s, the middle class has become more and more like the working class in terms of sexual
practices. The article "Sexual embourgeoisement? Social class
and sexual activity: 1938–1970" is an excellent starting point
and can be found in the February 1980 issue of the *American
Sociological Review*.

Chapter 4: "I Thought I Was Going to Die"

The fact that people in their 40s, 50s, and 60s are still
having sex is mainly a surprise to younger folks. However,
older black men still put a lot of emphasis on sexuality. One
interviewee was asked by his partner if he was secretly taking Viagra because she was impressed by his libido, stamina
and overall pipe-laying skills. While he was happy for the
compliment, he wasn't quite sure how to take it. Sort of
how a woman might feel being told that she looks good for
her age.

The research on sex and aging for men offers a complex picture. Men in their 50s report similar levels of satisfaction with their sex lives as men in their 20s, and more satisfaction than those in their 30s, presumably because they are less hung up, and more into the experience of sex than the act. The main issue reported by men is their sexual desires and the role of technology in addressing them. The two main technologies that shape men's sexual desires are the Internet and pharmacological drugs like Viagra. Sex trips overseas can be seen as the coming together of sexual fantasies linking power with desire and these technologies. For a fascinating discussion on the rise and role of Viagra in American culture, see Meika Loe's book *The Rise of Viagra: How the Little Blue Pill Changed Sex in America*.

Chapter 5: She Acts Like a Man

A lot has been written about how black women are characterized by white society as "Jezebels and Sapphires" (see Patricia Hill Collins for a comprehensive review). However, there has been less detailed analysis of black male attitudes toward women. In contrast, *machismo* has always been associated with patriarchal ideas of Latino men. While there is a long list of studies that focus on the attitudes of poor black men, very little has been produced on the attitudes of elite men. I attempt here to focus on men in general, and middle-class and professional black men in particular.

Research has highlighted the conflicted attitudes that black men have toward women's roles and place in society. More than two decades ago, Ransford & Miller's (1983) article "Race, Sex And Feminist Outlooks" showed that black males are more traditional in sex-role outlook than white males, especially those that identified themselves as middle class, and yet black females are not as "feminist." The real finding was not just that black males were found to be more traditional than whites, but that middle-class black men were more traditional than any other group in the study. In addition, further research has suggested that low black marriage rates may be more of a function of black men's attitudes than black women's attitudes. For a historical overview of the change in middle-class black men's attitudes, see Martin Summers, *Manliness and Its Discontents*.

One study of men who pay for prostitutes in Chicago called "Buying Sex: A survey of men in Chicago" demonstrated that it did not affect most men to know that women who were prostitutes were more likely to experience homelessness, were victims of violence, and start at a very young ages. 44% said that it would not change their attitude about paying for sex, while 42% said that it would matter. We can hope that this 42% can be impacted by information and advocacy. For an excellent critique of contemporary black male attitudes, see *New Black Man*, by Mark Anthony Neals; and a book by Bell Hooks titled *We Real Cool: Black Men and Masculinity*.

Chapter 6: The Frigid Black Woman

Julia Roberts can be a prostitute and still marry the rich man in *Pretty Woman*. Overall, white women are more likely to have a high number of partners than other women, but don't get stigmatized the way black women do. At the other extreme, the idea that black women are frigid is based on the idea that black women—and especially middle-class black women—are more sexually restrictive than other women. Some of the findings from *Sex In America* tend to confirm that African-American women are more sexually conservative than other groups of women, while black men tend to be more sexually adventurous than other groups of men. For a thorough examination of this "sexual mismatch" among black men and women, see Orlando Patterson, who based his analysis on the comprehensive National Health and Social Life Survey. For the most recent comparative data on sexual practices, see the September 15, 2005 Advanced Data from Vital and Health Statistics: "Sexual Behavior and Selected Health Measures: Men and Women 15–44 Years of Age, United States, 2002."

Chapter 7: Fat, Black, and Ugly

Most people know the story of the Hottentot Venus, the black woman from Africa brought to England to display aspects of her physical body that were considered different, such as her "protruding buttocks" and "elongated labia." After her death, her body was put on display in a museum. In a sense, black women's bodies have always been put on display. This chapter explores how that process is influenced by social class and black men.

Historian David Roediger provides an important insight

into the psychology of the minstrel tradition and the role it played in the minds of working-class white men. While historically black men have compared black women to white women, today, their physical stature is being compared to Brazilian women. The irony of course, is that most Brazilian women do not correspond with the myth of "ultimate beauty" that is often articulated. The recent article "Brazilian women too fat, men drink too much" suggested that more than 44% of women are overweight (http://www.reuters.com/article/healthNews/idUSN1426826620070314). For an important introspective view of black men's issue with size, see Scott Poulson-Bryants' book *Hung*.

Chapter 8: "She Knows How to Love Me"

The irony of Brazil with regard to African-Americans is that the country is often touted as an example of a society that has escaped the kind of racial divisions seen in the U.S. In *Neither Black Nor White*, Carl Degler provides a thorough examination of the historical development of racial patterns in Brazil and the United States. He argues that the main reason for the development of Brazil's alternative racial structure was the "mulatto escape hatch." The evolution of black-white sexual relations and the cultural differences in the position of Brazilian women created space for black men in Brazilian society in a way that was denied in America. For a detailed discussion of various aspects of Brazilian life and society see the special issue of *Daleus* (volume 129).

Chapter 9: "I'm Addicted!"

Playboy magazine started in 1953 and within a year became a staple of American culture. Recent books like *Pornified: How Pornography Is Transforming Our Lives, Our Relationships, and Our Families* point to the obvious fact that sex is all around us, most prominently in the virtual world. According to Donna Hughes in "The Internet and Sex Industries," in 1998, $1 billion was spent on adult content online in the U.S., making up 69% of total Internet sales. For information on the impact of pornography on young males, see Robert Jensen's book *Getting Off: Pornography and the End of Masculinity.*

Chapter 10: So This Is How It Feels to Be a White Man

When Cornel West described in *Race Matters* how it felt to be persistently passed by taxi-cabs on the streets of New York, he poignantly communicated the stigma of being both black and male. However, he did not communicate how it felt to be *Cornel West*, the famous public intellectual, and be discriminated against. How do accomplished black men deal with such status inconsistencies?

Researchers have shown that wealth differentials between whites and blacks are better indicators of economic disparities than income differentials. Middle class African Americans rely on jobs and occupational income for their financial status, whereas more whites can rely on resources like an inheritance and other assets (Oliver & Shapiro, 1995; Conley, 1999). In 1992, the median worth of elderly white men was $144,214 and for elderly white women was

$85,911. In stark contrast, the median worth of elderly black men was $16,091 and black women $15,452 (Ozawa and Tseng, 2000).

Chapter 11: Star Gazing

Why good men "go bad" is the essence of the "sex ratio" idea, which was fully explored in the book *Too Many Women*. The book illustrates a number of different ways that men act when faced with similar situations, and also suggests that there was a time when the sex ratio was actually worse than today, yet black men had higher marriage rates. Together, this shows that just because men have more options does not mean that they will take advantage of them. Men who inherit privilege are not condemned by their circumstances but by their lack of consciousness. The question for all men is how we act on our gender privilege.

Data on the earnings differential between black men and black women is from the American Community Survey, Tables B20005B and B20017B.

Chapter 12: "Sleep with a Girl from Morris Brown"

Ask a black male college student if he knows who Malcolm or Martin is. You don't even have to say last names—chances are he will look at you like you are crazy! Now ask him if he knows two of their notable female contemporaries and see what look you get. Now here comes the real rub—try and prove that it matters to his life. The point is not that man has to be feminist and know about the Violence Against Women Act or The Combahee River Collective Statement to be a "good man." In fact, my grandfather—who had a third grade education—is the best man I have ever known. But education is relative and can lead not to progressive attitudes, but to more sophisticated justifications of discrimination. Nobel winner James Watson's recent comments and books like *The Bell Curve* serve as a reminder that education does not always lead to more liberal ideas.

When it comes to gender and sexism, a similar assumption is held that the more educated a man is the more liberal or progressive his attitudes towards women are. However, education can actually reproduce rather than challenge inequality (Kane and Kyyro, 2001). Because college is one of the foundational places where the masculine, sexual, and racial identities of middle-class black men are developed, it behooves us to pay more attention to the issues that black college male students have while enrolled. This attention has to go deeper than recruitment and retention issues to explore what they are exposed to while they are on these campuses that will shape and sustain them in the future.

Chapter 13: "I Am Going to Take My Son"

Spike Lee's movie *Get on the Bus* captured the relationships and networks surrounding the Million Man March, in particular focusing on an estranged father and son using the trip as an opportunity to reconnect. The journey and the event of the Million Man March provided the occasion for these brothers to bond and find meanings in their life. It is not necessarily well known that the men that actually went to the march shows that they were mostly middle class. Upwards of 63% of the black men that attended the march had either some college education, were college graduates or had post graduate education. In addition, 33% had individual incomes between $30,000 and $49,000 per year and 36% made between $50,000 and $100,000 per year. For a critical discussion on the Million Man March, see Devon Carbados, *Black Men on Race, Gender, and Sexuality: A Critical Reader.*

On what basis do men bond? How do they try to bring younger men into manhood? Rites of passage for young white men during slavery involved having access to black women's bodies, the legacy of which is still with us today. W.E.B Dubois wrote, "I shall forgive the white South much in its final judgment day . . . but one thing I shall never forgive, neither in this world nor the world to come: its wanton and continued and persistent insulting of the black womanhood which it sought and seeks to prostitute to its lust." What will Brazilian men say of us in the future? (See *Men's Friendships* in the Research On Men And Masculinities Series for an overview on men and relationships.)

Chapter 14: Mantel Men

August Wilson is considered one of the greatest playwrights of the twentieth century. His Pittsburgh cycle explores the evolution of black life in Pittsburgh and is one of the most comprehensive portraits of black male life in the urban environment. In his last play, *Radio Golf*, Wilson introduced a character in the type of this new group of black male. As is often true, creative work on the topic seems to have come as late as social science or journalistic recognition.

Black writers have long worked to put forward more realistic portrayals of black men. Langston Hughes created the character Jesse B. Simple because he did not like the dominant images of black male protagonists. Ralph Ellison, Richard Wright, and many others have explored how black men are seen or not seen by white society. Increasingly, the question for some men is how the women in their lives see them. "Mantel Men" are struggling with the same type of objectification, ideation, or overall erasure of their personal identity captured in these earlier critiques.